We talk a lot about marital communication, but we often overemphasize the importance of marriage over that of the individual. But in a great marriage *you* matter too! When we're taking responsibility for our emotional, physical, mental, and spiritual well-being, we have love and grace enough to share. This book is all about including *you* in the equation of what it takes to make a marriage great!

> **JIM DALY,** president of Focus on the Family

We've been told there's no *I* in *team*, but we all know that thriving teams are made up of strong, competent *individuals*. The same is true in marriage. Are you a solid teammate right now? Or do you need to work through past hurts, learn to own your behavior, or address some crucial needs through self-care? *Empowered to Love* shows how targeted "personal training" can transform your life—as well as help you become the healthy, loving partner God intended.

> **DR. GREG SMALLEY,** vice president of marriage and family formation at Focus on the Family

In *Empowered to Love*, Bob and Tara reveal a way to bring hope, healing, guidance, and a deeper faith into your life and marriage. Their model has been tested and made stronger through their work with thousands of hurting and healthy couples. The principles in this resource will empower you in your home as well.

> **JOHN TRENT, Ph.D.,** president of StrongFamilies.com and coauthor of *Where Do I Go from Here?* (with Kari Trent Stageberg) and *The Blessing* (with Gary Smalley and Kari Trent Stageberg)

T0019091

Bob and Tara are more than just experts in their field; they reflect the message of personal health and responsibility in their own lives and marriages and through their work leading marriage intensives at Hope Restored. I have talked to countless couples around the country who didn't think their marriages had a future until they discovered the principles in this book. *Empowered to Love* is an excellent resource for anyone serious about caring for their own heart and marriage.

> **TED CUNNINGHAM,** senior pastor of Woodland Hills Family Church and author of *Fun Loving You*

It's so refreshing to read a marriage book that elevates the importance of health and well-being of the individual to be equal with the relationship. Bob and Tara focus on the importance of oneness and healthy separateness while providing a road map for creating a satisfying, fulfilling, and God-honoring marriage, complete with the practical tools and tips to pull it off. Be empowered to live and love well!

> **DR. TIM CLINTON,** president of the American Association of Christian Counselors and executive director of the Global Center for Mental Health, Addiction, and Recovery at Liberty University

I loved this book! Bob and Tara do an outstanding job of showing you what a healthy marriage looks like and then give you the practical tools to make it happen in your own life. Readers will discover that a healthy marriage begins when we first take responsibility to take care of our physical, mental, spiritual, and emotional health. Readers, God created you on purpose for a purpose. This is some life-changing content that brings hope and health to any marriage.

> **JIM BURNS, PhD,** president of HomeWord and author of *Doing Life with Your Adult Children*

In my four decades as a psychologist and professor, I've read many books about marriage. *Empowered to Love* is one of the most practical, realistic, and immediately applicable resources I've encountered. Bob and Tara accurately state that if individuals don't thrive, the marriage can't thrive. This unique focus on cultivating both individual health and the health of the marriage is an often overlooked yet absolutely essential requirement for growing a healthy, mutually satisfying, and God-honoring marriage.

> **DR. GARY OLIVER**, author or coauthor of over twenty books, including *It's All about Relationships* (with Dr. David H. Olson)

Tara and Bob have penned a great resource to empower spouses to love each other well. They bring years of up-close-and-personal counseling with couples who want to experience all that God has for them in marriage, and they now share their best practices to deepen real intimacy in our marriages. *Empowered to Love* is a great resource for couples who may sense that they are missing the mark on having the marriages they've always dreamed of. Read this book and allow these truths to sink into your spirit and heart.

> **DR. GARY AND BARB ROSBERG**, authors, speakers, and "America's Family Coaches"

Empowered to Love is a significant contribution to a growing body of resources showing that the best way to a strong marriage is by being the most mature person you can be. That's not easy, but Bob and Tara—leading voices in our understanding of what makes for a healthy marriage—are here to help.

> **RON DEAL**, speaker, podcaster, therapist, and bestselling author of *The Smart Stepfamily* and *Building Love Together in Blended Families* (with Dr. Gary Chapman)

Healthy marriages are *built*. In *Empowered to Love*, Bob and Tara use biblical insight and practical wisdom to provide a road map for a marriage that you and your spouse will both love. This book will help you love your mate and your marriage to the fullest!

JOHN LINDELL, lead pastor of James River Church in Springfield, Missouri

EMPOWERED

TO LOVE

Discovering Your

God-Given Power to Create

a Marriage You Both Love

ROBERT S. PAUL, MS
and TARA LALONDE, PHD

FOCUS
ON THE
FAMILY.

A Focus on the Family resource
published by Tyndale House Publishers

Empowered to Love: Discovering Your God-Given Power to Create a Marriage You Both Love
Copyright © 2024 by Focus on the Family. All rights reserved.

A Focus on the Family book published by Tyndale House Publishers, Carol Stream, Illinois 60188

Focus on the Family and the accompanying logo and design are federally registered trademarks of Focus on the Family, 8605 Explorer Drive, Colorado Springs, CO 80920.

Tyndale and Tyndale's quill logo are registered trademarks of Tyndale House Ministries.

Cover design by Eva M. Winters

Cover illustration of heart fire icon copyright © rashadashurov/Adobe Stock. All rights reserved.

Interior illustrations copyright © 2023 by Focus on the Family. All rights reserved.

Unless otherwise indicated, all Scripture quotations are from The ESV® Bible (The Holy Bible, English Standard Version®), copyright © 2001 by Crossway, a publishing ministry of Good News Publishers. Used by permission. All rights reserved. Scripture quotations marked NIV are taken from the Holy Bible, *New International Version,*® *NIV.*® Copyright © 1973, 1978, 1984, 2011 by Biblica, Inc.® Used by permission. All rights reserved worldwide. Scripture quotations marked NLT are taken from the *Holy Bible*, New Living Translation, copyright © 1996, 2004, 2015 by Tyndale House Foundation. Used by permission of Tyndale House Publishers, Carol Stream, Illinois 60188. All rights reserved.

For information about special discounts for bulk purchases, please contact Tyndale House Publishers at csresponse@tyndale.com, or call 1-855-277-9400.

ISBN 978-1-64607-113-5

Printed in the United States of America

30	29	28	27	26	25	24
7	6	5	4	3	2	1

Contents

Part 1

1

EMPOWERED
TO LOVE

YOU HAVE THE GOD-GIVEN POWER to make your marriage the best it can be. Over the years, we have seen many couples grab hold of this power and transform their struggling marriages. We've also seen couples who were doing well in their marriages learn to truly thrive, overflowing with love, fulfillment, and grace. What's beautiful is that the power to accomplish these things is, by God's grace, in your hands right now. You can take the first steps today to improve your marriage, even without your spouse's participation. But if both of you take hold of the power at your disposal, your marriage will become much better than either of you imagine.

Unfortunately, many couples miss out on the best that marriage can offer because they unknowingly put the proverbial cart before the horse. They say, "I do," and then they shift their focus to making their marriages great. At first glance, that might seem like a good approach, but it overlooks a fundamental truth: A marriage cannot thrive apart from the individuals in it. It can never be healthier or stronger than each spouse.

That doesn't mean a person needs to have it all together prior to getting hitched. Real marriages are composed of two imperfect people walking through this crazy world together. Growth and healing always take place over time, but the kind of growth and healing that lead to a stronger marriage must happen on an individual level.

Consider for a moment the lighting of a unity candle that is often included in modern weddings. During this little ceremony, the bride and groom each light a small candle, and then together they light a bigger candle in the middle of the table. The smaller candles represent their lives as individuals, and the larger candle represents their new relationship as a couple. After the unity candle is lit, they each blow out their smaller candles to symbolize shifting their focus from their individual lives to their marriage. This shift makes sense at first, but when the day-to-day realities of marriage set in, the results are disappointing, especially as time wears on. In fact, if a couple views marriage as leaving behind their individual selves to become a single entity, attending to their personal well-being might very well seem like time and energy *stolen* from the marriage. It might even seem contrary to godliness.

What couples so often miss is that a strong marriage is forged by seeking a healthy balance between caring for themselves as individuals and caring for the marriage as a whole, *not* choosing between the two. Fully embracing this critical balancing act can dramatically change the course of any marriage from one each spouse either likes well enough or is dissatisfied with to one that both are thrilled with.

In fact, our definition of a great marriage is "nothing less than two people *thrilled* with their relationship *and* the direction it is heading." Even if only one spouse is willing to do the hard work of strengthening the marriage, real progress can be made.

As radical as this may sound, we propose that the first step in making your marriage the best it can possibly be is to take radical responsibility for your own emotional, spiritual, physical, and mental well-being. This is the key to personal fulfillment and purpose—from a filled-up, empowered place, you will be perfectly positioned and equipped to invest meaningfully in your marriage and make it something special.

Initially it might sound as if we're encouraging self-centeredness and personal indulgence, reflecting the old adage *If it feels good, do it.* But this isn't our goal. Instead, we want to help you develop a balanced, biblically centered understanding of marriage. Many Christian couples have been taught a marriage strategy that denies self-care and emphasizes unhealthy selflessness and radical self-denial. Fortunately, we're not promoting either extreme. Rather than emphasizing the individual over the marriage or the marriage over the individual, we seek to equip you with a biblical view of marriage in which you and your spouse thrive as individuals and as a couple. God cares deeply about all three aspects of your marriage, and if any of them is neglected or hurt, He is not pleased!

If you're concerned that we might be missing the importance of sacrifice and selflessness in the Christian life, we want to put your mind at rest: We agree that a sacrificial investment in others is a central theme of Scripture. Later, we'll address how this fits into a balanced biblical approach to building a godly marriage. We believe this includes creating a relationship in which each of you is committed to the ultimate health and well-being of yourself, your spouse, *and* your marriage. Our marriages truly thrive when *all three* candles are burning brightly.

We certainly understand the tension in trying to balance self-care with the needs and interest of your spouse and your marriage. In fact, many years ago, my (Bob's) parents wrote a popular secular book that asked the question "Do I have to give up me to be loved by you?" Their strongly voiced answer was "No!" Our answer is similar, but with one significant difference: We also encourage loving, Christ-centered couples to make meaningful sacrifices for their spouses, their marriages, and their families. We view such sacrifices as *investments* that God calls faithful Christians to joyfully make while keeping self-care in clear focus as well.

How do you find that often elusive and delicate balance in your marriage? The ideal place to start is striving to become healthy, equipped, and empowered as an individual. Then, as you journey forward, you can add a generous investment in your spouse from a full storehouse while also investing in developing a great marital relationship.

With all these lofty goals in mind, our hope is that when you're done reading this book, you will

- have an empowered sense of what is within your control and a sense of freedom and release from what is not;
- see the many benefits of taking personal responsibility for yourself in all aspects of your life;
- have access to new ways of interacting with your spouse that feel safe for both of you;
- have some tools you can apply to improve your personal well-being and marriage, even if your spouse doesn't participate;
- find hope that even if your spouse doesn't consciously grow with you, your experience of marriage can improve; and

- see that even though you don't have the power to change your spouse, you do have great influence over how your spouse experiences your marriage.

Along the way, we'll share the stories and wisdom of six couples who courageously participated in Tara's research as part of Focus on the Family's Hope Restored marriage intensives. (The names of these couples and some details about their lives have been changed to maintain their anonymity.)

Since this book isn't just for married couples in crisis, we'll also be sharing examples of how this material applies to couples who are generally doing well. We hope you'll find something impactful in the stories and principles presented that you can personally apply. We are so passionate about this material that we'll even share aspects of our unique journeys, including some of our successes and failures. Like you, each of us is on a journey of discovery as we seek to understand more fully God's design for marriage. We're interested not just in teaching theory but also in applying the concepts and principles in our own lives and marriages. We would never present them here if we couldn't make them work personally.

We wholeheartedly believe that our Lord deeply desires and is committed to our health and well-being—personally and relationally—through the end of time. Each of us is seeking to align our lives more closely with His design as empowered individuals married to other empowered individuals, fully equipped to love well.

A Bit about Your Authors

Before we embark on this journey together, we'd like to tell you a little about ourselves. We both have a passion for seeing couples thrive in their marriages, in part because of our unique journeys. As you'll see, we've each had our fair share of challenges, disappointments, and growth opportunities as we've sought to become the people God created us to be while striving to have thriving marriages. No small undertaking!

Additionally, as part of Focus on the Family, we have the freedom to overtly refer to God and Scripture in our work and teaching. This isn't always the case for those in private practice. By working predominantly with Christians, we can bring God's Word and perspective into our counseling, which allows for greater empowerment and success not only for the couples we seek to help but also for us. We're excited we can do that here, too!

Robert Paul's Story

My parents married young, and I was conceived right away. Neither of them was ready for the level of responsibility that parenting required. This was especially true of my father, who struggled to figure out who he was and how to be an adult. Within my first year of life, my parents separated and went through an ugly and contentious divorce soon after. Neither of them had any religious convictions or faith in God. They simply tried their best to make it on their own.

When I was three years old, my mom married a wonderful man who accepted me and raised me as his own. My biological father was still in my life, but at first I saw him only every other weekend. When I was five, he married a woman who treated me with tremendous love and devotion. These two couples—my mom and her new husband, and my father and his new wife—were extremely different from one another and didn't get along very well. The tension between them was often intense, but all four treated me well. So I hopped back and forth between the two households and watched both families grow over the years, with five half-siblings entering the scene.

In my teens, I became a musician and eventually got caught up in the stereotypical rock-star lifestyle filled with reckless excess. By my late teens and early twenties, though, I began to see the emptiness of where I was headed, especially after witnessing the impact of tragic events on some of my friends. I sensed that truth existed beyond the empty mess I saw in the lives of so many, and I started searching for it. But I had one stipulation: That truth could not be found in Jesus. I didn't like Christians, and I certainly didn't want to be one. But God knew better!

One day I bumped into a beautiful and fascinating woman who (fortunately for me) had just found her way back to her Christian faith. Jenni was on fire for the Lord!

Although we connected immediately, we also had strong and stubborn personalities, and we fought about religion more than anything else. But Jenni's strength of character and God's pursuit of my heart eventually won out. In a dramatic and (I believe) miraculous way, she and the Holy Spirit helped me find my way to the truth, and I accepted Jesus as Lord of my life the day before our wedding.

Over the next few years, our faith grew stronger, but each of us brought a lot of baggage into the marriage. Our biggest challenge was probably my unrecognized codependency. I'd entered our marriage believing what I had been taught: that as a husband, I was supposed to identify and meet all my wife's needs, and she was supposed to identify and meet all mine. I thought we should love and care for each other's hearts and be willing to adjust who we were (our personhood) and how we lived (our behavior and habits) to avoid upsetting each other.

As a result of those false ideas (and a bunch more), we struggled in our marriage for nearly thirty years! As of this writing, Jenni and

I have been married more than forty-three years, and we agree that the last twelve have been amazing. As you might guess, many of the principles discussed in this book, as well as a sizable amount of grace, patience, and guidance from our loving Lord, were responsible for our personal and relational transformation.

I'm excited to share with you what Jenni and I have been learning throughout our journey together. And after sharing these principles with thousands of other couples, I'm confident this stuff really works!

Tara Lalonde's Story

My mother was Anglican, and my father was Baptist, and when they married in the late 1960s, they tried to find a church both of them could feel comfortable in. But they quickly gave up and let their faith take a back seat to the busyness of work and raising two daughters. I was fourteen when my dad had a crisis in his life that prompted his return to the Lord. At that point, my parents found a nondenominational church that felt good to both of them, and we started going to church regularly from then on.

My own faith journey had a bumpy beginning. As a child and young adult, I acknowledged Jesus as my Savior, but I wasn't ready for Him to rule my life. I figured I had secured my place in heaven and avoided "the other place," so wasn't that good enough? It wasn't until I was twenty-four—alone, disillusioned, and experiencing mild depression—that I turned from "my way" and made Jesus the Lord of my life. Over the next six years, I slowly drew closer to God, coming to understand who He really was and how He loved me more than I could ever imagine. At a particularly significant crossroads early in that journey, I made a difficult decision to follow God's will for my life instead of marrying a non-Christian man I deeply loved.

That was a profound turning point for me. My way had not worked, and I had finally drawn a line in the sand. From that moment on, I began living my life devoted to growing in my faith and surrendering my life and my way of doing things to God. Over and over He showed up and blew me away. My regular prayer for almost a decade was *Less of me and more of You.*

At thirty I met my husband, Vince, and we were married a couple of months before my thirty-second birthday. I had been single for six years and had settled into being an adult on my own. Vince had married very early in his twenties and was going through a divorce when we met. By that time, I was just finishing my master of divinity degree, with a major in professional counseling. I explored with Vince what had happened in his first marriage, and we agreed that we did not want that to happen to us. He was aware of how his indifference toward the marriage, along with his tendency toward controlling behavior, contributed to the breakdown of that relationship, and he seemed committed to doing things differently.

Vince's tendencies were concerning to me, but after spending a weekend in a silent retreat with God, I felt He was asking me to go forward with marrying Vince. I also felt quite sure that we were going to have significant challenges, at least at first. It wasn't clear how long these struggles would last.

When Vince and I married, the challenges began almost immediately. My husband's tendencies returned, and I began a journey with the Lord of learning to care for my heart when I didn't feel Vince's care for me. I also learned to release my husband and his journey to the Lord.

Over the years, things have improved, and I have come to understand more about Vince's personality and my own. We are very different people! He looks at the world in a highly structured and precise way. He believes the world has an intended order, so when life is out of order or things aren't as he thinks they should be, he becomes visibly frustrated. Why anyone would accept imperfection or a lack of precision makes no sense to him.

I, on the other hand, don't prioritize or value precision the way Vince does. In fact, I suspect I have a learning disability that makes this sort of precision in areas that aren't important to me almost impossible. I just can't make my brain value things it doesn't see. I am relational and can make sense of very complex relational patterns, but details like turning down the thermostat before I leave for work don't seem to stick no matter how hard I try.

From childhood experiences, I also came to believe that I was never good enough for the people in my life. I always expected to be set aside or treated as if I had no value. I wasn't aware of these hidden beliefs until a few years ago, but they were the guiding principle in all my adult relationships. Imagine my surprise when I finally saw it!

Professionally, psychotherapy is my second career. I started a private practice in my early thirties and earned my PhD while working full-time. I centered my doctoral dissertation on researching six couples who had gone through Focus on the Family's Hope Restored marriage intensives. At the time, the first three couples were using the tools they had learned about to strengthen their lives and marriages. The other three were still struggling or heading for divorce. I wondered why. The results of that research ignited in me a desire to help struggling spouses. I wanted more couples to use these helpful tools to improve their lives and marriages.

As my career progressed, I also developed a deep understanding of trauma and a commitment to helping individuals who had experienced single-incident trauma and complex childhood trauma. My passion today is twofold: (1) empowering couples to find happiness and fulfillment personally and in their marriages and (2) helping individuals heal from past trauma that robs them of becoming the grounded adults God created them to be. Naturally, these two passions are often intertwined.

Let Our Journey Begin

Many couples we've worked with express the need for resources to help them care well for themselves, for their spouses, and for their marriages. This book will equip you with those resources. When you grab hold of the principles we present, your experience of marriage can change for the better, even if your everyday circumstances seem to be the same!

In the following chapters, we'll provide time-tested tools you can use to improve your marriage as you work toward greater health and wholeness as an individual. We believe that as more of us become empowered to love, others will see the difference in our lives and will want what we have.

Our grand vision is that couples everywhere will learn the art of caring well for themselves and their spouses and then share these skills with others, so that marriages around the world can become glorious examples of what is possible with Christ.

2

FOUNDATIONS OF
A GREAT MARRIAGE

COUNTLESS BOOKS HAVE BEEN WRITTEN about how to achieve intimacy in marriage. Many contain great ideas, but they often miss the foundational elements that empower couples to build a satisfying and fulfilling marriage. In this chapter, we'll introduce these elements and build upon them in the rest of this book.

First, we'll show you how to make your relationship feel like the safest place on earth emotionally, spiritually, physically, and mentally. When a marriage feels safe, it becomes a sanctuary for you and your spouse, a place each of you can run to after a day of slaying dragons. A marriage like that refreshes and recharges you so you can wake up every day ready to face whatever life throws your way.

How do you create a marital safe harbor? Not surprisingly, it begins with your individual journeys toward health and wholeness.

Ideally, as each of you embraces your own journey, you will have something valuable to contribute to the construction and maintenance of your relational retreat. What this looks like can vary greatly from couple to couple because people refresh and recharge differently.

Second, we've noticed that problems and disappointments in marriage are generally the result of misplaced responsibilities—either taking responsibility for things that aren't ours to take or not taking responsibility for things that are. Fully embracing personal responsibility is the key to empowerment. *Not* taking personal responsibility or attempting to take responsibility for things outside our control inevitably leads to frustration, disappointment, and bondage. In fact, it can jeopardize our sense of peace. Who hasn't heard the Serenity Prayer? "God, grant me the serenity to accept the things I cannot change, the courage to change the things I can, and the wisdom to know the difference."[1]

Next, we'll focus on understanding how a marriage should be structured. We've found this confuses many couples. Structure is about much more than roles and responsibilities, although it includes these aspects. If you were to ask some average people to draw a picture of a healthy marriage, most would give you a blank stare (and a blank piece of paper). Everybody has some ideas about what might be included, but actually drawing a picture of it? How would you even begin to do that?

Since "God is love" (1 John 4:8) and the best Christian marriages are infused with an abundance of God and His love, we'll briefly share our understanding of how He can accomplish this in our marriages. No discussion of the foundations of a great marriage would be complete without it!

Finally, we'll conclude the chapter with some results from my (Tara's) dissertation research. What I discovered was a key motivation for this book.

A Foundation of Safety

Why is it important to begin this exploration of marital foundations with a focus on safety? Most couples don't physically abuse
each other, so they tend to think they have that part covered—"We
never hit each other, so our marriage is safe, isn't it?" But safety
is about so much more than physical safety, as essential as that is.

All humans have an innate, God-designed need for meaningful
connection, or intimacy. Our hearts yearn to feel close to someone. But for that connection to occur, two people must open up
and let each other in. Physical connection is essential for healthy
relationships, but we are so much more than physical beings. God
created us as complex beings, and the most satisfying, intimate
connections occur when we experience each other with our whole
being—emotionally, spiritually, mentally, *and* physically.

The risk, however, is that the moment we let someone get close
to us in these ways, we instantly become vulnerable. The deeper
the connection, the closer the other person gets to the places
within us that are easily damaged. To amplify the risk, the more
we care about someone, the more vulnerable we are to being hurt.
This is why intimacy feels so difficult and risky.

Unfortunately, if we don't feel safe enough to welcome intimacy
in our marriages, our ability to stay connected with our spouses
shuts off, and we shut down. Like turning off a light switch, when
the human nervous system senses danger (or potential danger),
it shuts down our brains' ability to connect, and we move from
thinking to reacting. We suddenly find ourselves on high alert and
protectively jump into fight, flight, or freeze mode in a fraction
of a second.

When we sense that the danger has passed, the thinking and
connecting parts of our brains come back online, and we can

evaluate whether it is safe enough to connect again. Unfortunately, by then we may have missed the opportunity. This process occurs quickly, naturally, and unconsciously for the most part. It's how we were built to remain safe. When we feel seriously threatened or even moderately at risk, our brains flip to alert mode. All our brains care about are survival and safety. The moment for real connection is gone.

Opening up and allowing someone you care about to know you deeply can make you feel vulnerable. And it gets even more complicated if you had painful or disappointing relational inter-actions growing up—and who among us hasn't in this fallen world? When that's the case, your fear of getting hurt again can be easily triggered. The more frequent or intense those interactions were, the more difficult it may become to open up and stay open long enough to meaningfully connect with your spouse. You may become more sensitive to perceived danger and close up for long periods of time. Trust can become a constant challenge. It can even be difficult to stay open to God's love long enough to receive His encouragement and help. But when you make safety a priority in all aspects of your marriage, you and your spouse will begin to relax, open up, and connect with each other.

Creating personal and relational safety is the fastest and easi-est way to set the stage for a deeply satisfying, intimate marriage. Unfortunately, very few couples we encounter have made safety the top priority in every area of their marriage. But we know that "safety first" works!

We are passionate about searching for anything that reveals God's original design and intent for life and marriage. Everything goes much better when we live in harmony with God versus being at odds with Him. Prior to humanity's fall, God created us to live in peace and safety in the Garden, where we would be relaxed, open, and connected. But in the harsh reality of living in a fallen world, how can you create a relationship that approximates God's original design? How can you make your marriage a safe place where you can get refreshed and recharged?

It all starts with *you*!

Responsibility and Power, Responsibility and Freedom

Creating a secure marital garden begins with each individual in the relationship. Personal responsibility is our primary source of power and freedom and the key to our ultimate success in marriage! It's also how we were designed to live when we exit childhood, as well as how we acquire the corresponding benefits of effective, fully functional "adulting."

Personal responsibility simply means embracing the fact that you are in charge of your emotional, spiritual, physical, and mental well-being. (We'll use the abbreviation *ESPM* to help us remember these areas.) Accepting personal responsibility doesn't mean you are necessarily good at it. *Yet*. Learning to care well for yourself generally improves with time, attention, and practice. But adulthood isn't attained until you become capable of full, responsible self-care and accept the job going forward, even before you're skilled at it. Then as you become more skilled in caring well for yourself, it leads to power and freedom. How could that be bad?

When Jesus was asked which of the commandments was the most important, He quoted Deuteronomy 6:5: "'Love the LORD your God with all your heart and with all your soul and with all your mind and with all your strength.' The second is this: 'Love your neighbor as yourself.' There is no commandment greater than these" (Mark 12:30-31, NIV). In referencing this Scripture, Jesus was saying that we need to love God with our *whole* being, which He broke down into four areas of personhood. (Sounds like ESPM, doesn't it?) So when you love God with every bit of who you are, you are following His greatest commandment. God created you to love Him with all your heart, soul, mind, and strength. And loving the One who created you means caring for all aspects of yourself.

Loving God through embracing personal responsibility is what enables you to love others well. *But this is nearly impossible if you don't understand that you are lovable or if you don't care for yourself on a regular basis.* If your tank is empty, you have nothing to give. And you can't give what you don't have. But when your tank is full, you can give generously and make a meaningful difference in a world that is in desperate need.

Healthy adults not only take responsibility for their ESPM well-being; they also evaluate themselves regularly to see how they're doing in the four areas of personhood. When you, as an empowered, responsible adult, feel a bit low or neglected in any of these areas, *you* do something about it. If needed or desired, you can receive help from others, as long as you maintain a firm grip on your responsibility and remember that you alone have the power to get the job done. Certainly, your spouse could help you. But if your spouse isn't available to lend a hand or can't help in the way you want or need, you must remember that you are the only person, with God's help, who retains the ability and resources to fill up your tank. The power to care for yourself remains squarely in your hands.

Unfortunately, most of us have developed less-than-ideal ways of managing self-care. This is particularly true when we're under stress. Many of our coping strategies were developed in childhood and more or less worked because we were young and had limited options. But these strategies eventually became well-rehearsed habits that we continue to rely on as adults, even if they're ineffective. We just respond in the ways we always have without giving much thought to what we're actually doing.

Fortunately, we aren't stuck with our immature ways of coping. We can discover and develop more mature ways of caring for ourselves, even in stressful situations. Our brains can be healed and rewired to better function as healthy, responsible adult brains, allowing us to attend to our ESPM elements. Obviously, how to pull this off becomes critically important, and we'll explore ways we can implement more mature self-care strategies later in the book.

What Does a Healthy Marriage Look Like?

Next, let's turn our attention to understanding what a healthy marriage looks like. Starting with the idea of a responsible, empowered adult, we'll construct a diagram of a healthy marriage piece by piece.

As we discussed earlier, a responsible, empowered adult is committed to growing in health and wholeness as an individual. This is the foundation of any satisfying, intimate marriage. So even though our spouses may meet some of our ESPM needs, we are ultimately responsible for our well-being in these areas. The responsibility is right where it belongs.

Blaming our spouses for not meeting our needs saps our power and sets us up to fail. God created us to take ownership of our growth and well-being. He's not likely to accept our excuses, such as "My wife didn't help me with that . . ." or "What was I supposed to do when my husband . . . ?" God is more interested in how we live our lives and respond in the most challenging circumstances. He cares about how well each of us is caring for the temple He has entrusted to us. The apostle Paul wrote, "Do you not know that your bodies are temples of the Holy Spirit, who is in you, whom you have received from God? You are not your own; you were bought at a price. Therefore honor God with your bodies" (1 Corinthians 6:19-20, NIV).

So the first element in our diagram of a healthy marriage is personal responsibility. We'll depict this by drawing a circle with a dotted line around each spouse representing each individual's responsibility for their ESPM well-being. The line is dotted rather than solid to represent our ability to be open enough for meaningful connection with others. God has designed us for healthy, satisfying relationships with one another, and truly healthy adults also have an active, ongoing connection with the source of life itself, our Lord Jesus Christ.

A Whole, Healthy Adult Who Is Well Cared For

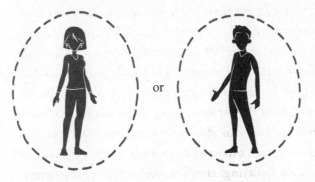

or

1. Emotionally
2. Spiritually
3. Physically
4. Mentally

Built on this foundation of personal responsibility is a healthy romantic relationship between a man and a woman who are fully functioning, responsible, and empowered adults, each of whom has a life-giving relationship with Christ. The biblical concept of intimacy, at its core, is the journey of two people getting to know each other in deeper ways over a period of time. This concept is based on the Hebrew word *yada*, which is usually translated "to know deeply" and often describes an intimate bond.

The following diagram shows the initial stages of developing a healthy relationship between a man and a woman:

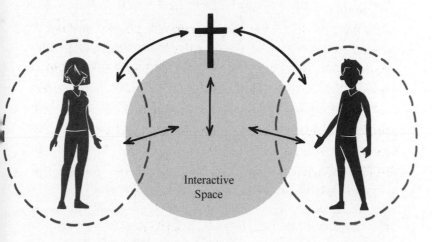

Notice that we've added a larger circle in the middle of this diagram (with arrows pointing to each individual space). This middle circle is called the *interactive space*. All healthy relationships include an ongoing series of interactions between two people. Both individuals in the relationship have their own personal space and ideally are taking good care of themselves so they'll stay healthy and well cared for. However, they can also enter the interactive space to actively engage with each other. If they want their relationship to be meaningful and satisfying, they'll actively find ways to make that middle circle a space where they can both feel safe and enjoy each other's company. It will become a place they'll look forward to entering and spending time.

For a relationship to be truly safe and respectful, however, each person will enter the other person's private circle only when they're invited, and they will leave politely whenever asked. Even as a relationship moves toward deeper intimacy, personal responsibility continues. As mentioned earlier, we are most vulnerable when we let someone get close to us, so we have a responsibility to protect our hearts. For this reason, access to the most valuable and vulnerable parts of ourselves must be by invitation only. Without these important boundaries in place, feeling truly safe in a relationship is virtually impossible. The author of Proverbs wisely said, "Above all else, guard your heart, for everything you do flows from it" (4:23, NIV).

Some individuals abdicate their responsibility to care for themselves, and the other person in the relationship willingly accepts that responsibility. But as generous as it might seem, doing for someone what God intended for that person to do for themselves is neither helpful nor respectful. Instead, it enables them to stay functionally like a child instead of grabbing hold of their God-given power.

When invited, we can enter another person's private circle to lovingly *assist* them, but we need to be careful not to take *responsibility* for that person's ESPM well-being. Helping one another is a wonderful aspect of God's design for meaningful relationships, but accepting and assuming personal responsibility for taking care of ourselves is central to our power as adults. The only exception, of course, would be if one person is incapable of fully caring for themselves because of an illness or injury.

As a romantic relationship between a man and a woman grows and deepens, they often reach an important moment of decision. The deeper their connection becomes, the closer they get to the treasures God has placed in each of us. These treasures are not only of incalculable worth, but they are also easily devalued and damaged. Each individual must ask, *Should I open up and share the most sacred and precious parts of myself with this person?*

Before one person gives another person access to those treasures, God provides an additional layer of protection for the relationship: a *covenant*. As in the Temple in Jerusalem, access to the more sacred parts of ourselves is meant to be restricted. This covenant protection is depicted in our diagram as an outer circle with a solid line. This completed diagram is referred to as the Healthy Marriage Model.

Covenant Marriage Boundary

Interactive Space

Scripture tells us that the covenant (a promise or vow) between a husband and a wife is meant to reflect the marital covenant between Christ (the Bridegroom) and His bride (the church): "'Therefore a man shall leave his father and mother and hold fast to his wife, and the two shall become one flesh.' This mystery is profound, and I am saying that it refers to Christ and the church" (Ephesians 5:31-32).

God's covenant with His church is a promise of confidence and security. We know we can count on Him to be there with us and for us, no matter what. Scripture encourages us to "be strong and courageous. Do not fear or be in dread of [those who seek to harm you], for it is the LORD your God who goes with you. He will not leave you or forsake you" (Deuteronomy 31:6). Likewise, the marital covenant between a man and a woman is meant to create a supremely safe environment, a space where we can be known in the deepest and most vulnerable ways without fear or regret.

This model of a healthy marriage is a rich representation of God's intended design that we'll refer to periodically throughout the remainder of this book. (You can also find a more complete discussion of the Healthy Marriage Model in *9 Lies That Will Destroy Your Marriage* by Robert Paul and Greg Smalley.)

The Good News about Love

Many of the clients who come to us for marriage counseling say things like "I no longer love my spouse" or "There's no love left in our marriage." The sentiment expressed is that love is almost mystical, the result of a complicated combination of attraction, chemistry, and numerous strategies aimed at keeping love alive and the fires of passion burning. A common accompanying belief is that once love is gone and the flame goes out, there is really no way to get them back.

Some Christians will counter with the idea that love is not really a *feeling* at all but rather a *commitment* to act in loving ways regardless of how we feel. From this perspective, loving feelings are seen as nice but unnecessary. Husbands and wives are to remain true to their call to love, whether or not any loving feelings are present.

The debate about whether love is a feeling or a commitment can become heated, and both sides are passionate about their positions. Such arguments usually end in a stalemate.

So which is it?

We believe that love is a commitment *and* a feeling. Certainly, taking our vows seriously as followers of Christ is critical for creating an intimate, safe marital environment. There is no other healthy way for that interactive space to be a sanctuary we can run to for rest and recharging. However, feelings of love are a wonderful gift from God. We believe they're meant to be an ongoing source of energy and joy for married couples.

What does one do when the feelings are hard to find or seem as if they're gone forever? Understanding what love is—and how God created it to work—can provide the answer.

The reality is that no human being can generate love. We can't manufacture a single drop of it. Yet it isn't magical or mystical. First John 4:8 states quite clearly, "God is love." Thus, there is no genuine love apart from God, period! Every true feeling or expression of love comes directly from God, whether or not the individuals involved recognize it. Love comes from God to us, and then we have the opportunity to drink it in deeply, receive its blessings, and generously share it with others.

Since many cultures view the heart as the gateway to love, and the Bible often mentions the importance of the heart in love and faith, it can be a useful reference point to help us better understand God and His love. We like to view the heart as having two doors—a top door that connects a person to God, our source, and a front door that connects us to other people. You may not be the creator of love, but you are the responsible keeper of the doors to your heart. God has given you the freedom to decide when and how often you open and close these doors. If the top door is closed, you will be cut off from the source of love—love will be absent, and you will suffer that loss. If the front door is closed, an exchange of love between you and others will be absent, and you will be cut off from the important component of human connection.

The good news is that the power to open and close the doors are completely within your control. If you open the top door, God won't hesitate to pour His love into your heart. You can drink it in deeply as it fills and saturates your entire being. As long as that door is open, God (who *is* love) is there in plentiful supply. Then, as desired, you can open the front door to others and share God's love generously and sacrificially. We say "sacrificially" because as you share God's love, there is often a cost. Your supply of His love may feel exhausted. But since you have the ability to remain connected to God and His *endless* supply, you can continually refill your heart's capacity to love others.

So when husbands and wives tell us that "the fire is gone" in their marriages, our response is that they have somehow shut their top door and are not receiving God's love for that person. That is the only possible reason a person no longer feels love for their spouse. There are many reasons why someone might choose to close that door, but God has given each of us the ability, freedom, and responsibility to be the doorkeepers to our hearts. Becoming responsible doorkeepers is a fundamental component of being empowered to love.

The Difference between Success and Failure

In my (Tara's) dissertation research, I interviewed six couples who attended Hope Restored marriage intensives at one of our Focus on the Family locations one year prior to meeting with me. All six couples initially found the program helpful and felt hopeful for the future of their marriages when they left their intensives. But as time passed, many couples had different experiences using the techniques they learned at Hope Restored. I specifically chose three couples who were using the tools and said things were getting better, and three other couples who were struggling or had given up. My basic research question to all of them was *Why?* I asked open-ended questions and then sorted through what they reported while looking for similarities and patterns.

To my surprise, very clear themes emerged. Both groups shared similar patterns after their intensives, but the most glaring difference was that the couples whose marriages were improving had taken personal responsibility for practicing the techniques they'd learned and were intentional about deepening their individual faith journeys. The couples who continued to struggle acknowledged that they were *not* taking responsibility to do those things.

Many other marriage studies over the years have had similar findings: One major key to successfully turning around a troubled marriage is taking personal responsibility. From there, one person enhances their progress by intentionally using the tools they've learned while growing in their faith. This combination appears to unlock the power to experience greater degrees of fulfillment and happiness, even if only one spouse is participating in the process.

Bill, one of the husbands from the successful group focused on personal responsibility, became intentional about his relationship with God, and kept using the tools on his own for the first nine months while his wife reverted to struggling with pain and resentment. Previously, they had lived independent and unhappy lives until Bill had had an affair, which had led them to a Hope Restored marriage intensive. Prior to that, he had been a workaholic, and Sadie had struggled with depression and health issues. She felt that Bill had abandoned her, and initially she wasn't ready to accept the changes in her husband. For nine months, her pain kept her reacting in protective and aggressive patterns, and then her thinking finally shifted and she began taking personal responsibility for her own healing as well.

Bill admitted, "I was always directing the blame back at Sadie for everything. When I focused on making it not about what she did or didn't do, it opened up the way for us to heal and not constantly be so antagonistic."

In our work with couples at the marriage intensives, the idea of personal responsibility is often one of the biggest stumbling blocks to success. Based on thousands of couples' testimonies, as well as our own experiences of using the tools in our marriages, we know the tools work *if we use them*. Problems arise, however, when one or both individuals in a marriage remain more focused on whether their spouse is using the tools than accepting responsibility for using the tools themselves. As the unsuccessful couples in my research illustrate, there is no power in that.

Unlike Bill, Andrew and Cindy continued to focus on their differences and the lack of change in their spouse. I remember how defeated Andrew seemed when he said, "What else can I do, you know? It's just that it takes two people, and she's not willing to work at it." He didn't realize the power he had within himself and gave up trying just as his wife had. Sadly, one thing is certain: If no one is working to make things better, nothing will change. Nothing will improve.

Even so, when even one person grabs hold of their God-given power and leans in, amazing things can happen.

3

IDENTITY
AND PURPOSE

IN THE PREVIOUS CHAPTER, we introduced the importance of remaining deeply connected to God so you can be fully empowered to love your spouse. But what happens after you become empowered to love? What is the point or purpose of all that power?

As a child of God and a servant of Christ, you can be certain that the ultimate purpose of your life goes far beyond your own pleasure and fulfillment. As much as God loves you and wants nothing but the best for you, He's got a lot going on in the world, and it appears He wants His children to be a big part of what He is doing. As God said to the prophet Jeremiah, "Before I formed you in the womb I knew you, and before you were born I consecrated you" (Jeremiah 1:5).

Your appearance on this planet was not in any way accidental or random. God created you on purpose for a purpose. Regardless of what it may look like to others, He has something grand in mind for you. Even though humans share many characteristics, each of us is unique and intentionally designed for a specific purpose. Our Lord is our *perfect* craftsman, and He never makes mistakes: "For we are God's handiwork, created in Christ Jesus to do good works, which God prepared in advance for us to do" (Ephesians 2:10, NIV).

Okay, that sounds great in theory. *Perfectly crafted . . . whatever!* In my thirties, I (Bob) regularly complained to God about my perceived shortcomings and design flaws. I was always comparing myself with others, especially other men. Plenty of men seemed to have so much more going for them than I did. I was convinced they were much better equipped to make a real difference in the Kingdom. I, on the other hand, had so many limitations and issues that I felt a long way from being perfectly crafted. With all these issues, how in the world would God be able to use me in any meaningful way—and why would He want to?

When I became a Christian, I was rescued from my impending doom, and my heart's desire was transformed. I just wanted to serve God well and be useful and pleasing to Him. In church, though, I kept hearing messages that confused me. Sometimes it seemed as if I was a horrible sinner who was going to get into heaven only by the grace-filled skin of my teeth. But other messages talked about how much God loved me and thought I was awesome. Now, I didn't think I was all that bad, but I knew I wasn't awesome. So I regularly complained to the Lord. After all, He had the ability to make me any way He wanted, so why didn't He make me more like Joe or Peter or Steve? Why didn't He make me like a whole host of men I knew who seemed to have more of what I wanted? With some of those qualities, I would be able to do something special and make a real difference in the world.

Finally, a very patient God made clear to me that He had heard my complaints, and He acknowledged my dissatisfaction.

Bob, I realize that you aren't pleased with how I made you. It appears you think I could have done better, I felt Him saying to me. This may come as a surprise to you, but you weren't on the design committee when I made you, and I didn't need your help. And unlike you, I am quite pleased with My design. I may not have made you like Joe or Peter or Steve, but that wasn't My intent. I made you perfectly as I intended, completely designed for the role and work I have for you in My Kingdom. So if you really want to please Me, as you say, then just be the best Bob you can be, and I will be completely satisfied. You may not be able to do what Joe or Peter or Steve can do, but I created them for that. You, on the other hand, are perfectly created to do what I brought you here to do.

Well, that got my attention. On the one hand, I felt the Lord scolding me. On the other hand, I was completely humbled. Furthermore, I felt loved and affirmed. And beyond all that, I felt empowered and free. You see, I really can't be a great Joe, Peter, or Steve, but I can be the best Bob Paul on the planet. And if that is what God is asking of me—to be the best Bob Paul I can be—I am certainly set up to succeed. From that point on, I wanted to do everything in my power to understand who He created me to be and what He created me to do, and then be and do it to the best of my ability. For more than thirty years now, that has been my overarching goal and desire.

EXERCISE

Spend some time thinking about how you see yourself.
What does your perspective look like? Are you comparing
yourself with other people and using those comparisons to
measure the value of how God designed you? What might
it look like to surrender your perspective to Him and begin
exploring what God sees and plans for you? Would you be
willing to accept His design and live freely as the person He
created you to be?

Sometimes we have an idea that the purpose of our lives should
be to make a grand impact on the world, but we miss the more
profound purpose of simply living for an audience of one. Perhaps
God's greatest desire for each of us is to love Him more and to love
others well. Maybe your most important role is to impact one person for God so they will go on to impact many more people. We
may want to make a big impact in this life, but often the small things
we do ripple into eternity in ways we'll never know about this side
of heaven. But how great a day it will be when we hear our heavenly
Father say, "Well done, good and faithful servant! You have been
faithful with a few things; I will put you in charge of many things.
Come and share your master's happiness!" (Matthew 25:23, NIV).

Embracing the Adventure

Once you've acknowledged and accepted the reality that God created you exactly as He intended, the next step is getting to know
yourself. To be done well, this must involve more than simply
making a list of what you already know about yourself and then
superimposing your judgments and evaluations of each trait. That's

what we're doing when we complain to God that we want more than what He's given us. The journey of self-discovery involves getting to know yourself as God knows you—your gifts and skills, your inclinations and potential. It's possible you've not yet identified and uncovered some of these traits, but once you start to see yourself as God sees you, you'll be much better positioned for maximum empowerment and success.

People have a variety of reactions when we stress the importance of getting to know themselves better. Some feel the process is self-indulgent and self-centered—*Shouldn't we focus on the needs of others instead and remain committed to serving God and His people?* Others seem afraid of what they'll uncover if they look too deeply. Still others don't seem interested in spending the time and energy needed to do this work. However, we are convinced that to find and fulfill God's perfect will for your life and to experience the deepest levels of contentment and fulfillment in your marriage, it's essential that you invest time in focused self-reflection. A little introspection goes a long way.

Once you've accepted the value and importance of self-reflection, you'll begin to know yourself more fully and see yourself as God sees you. Self-reflection can also energize and inspire your relationship with God, which can substantially transform your relationship with your spouse.

Instead of trying to be who others say you are or who you think you should be, work on becoming who God created you to be. Seeing yourself through God's eyes and understanding yourself from His perspective will bring greater clarity and focus to your life. It can also give you the courage to say yes or no without guilt. There is great freedom in just being yourself! It equips you to develop good relationships and make the unique impact in this world that you were created for.

A Little More Romance, Please

Do you want a life filled with romance and passion? Do you like the idea of having a little more adventure? It may come as a surprise, but you actually possess the power to create romance, passion, and adventure in your life. We know from personal experience how this works.

How can you get that power? First, let's discuss romance in general and some of the misconceptions many of us have. Most people would love to have more romance in their lives, but even their best efforts fall short. This is particularly true for the average guy. Contrary to the belief of many wives we talk to, most husbands are actually very interested in having more romance and passion in their lives and marriages. But one thing we've learned about men is that typically they hate to fail. In fact, they often avoid or quit any endeavor if they don't believe they can succeed.

Many men we've worked with say they've tried to foster more romance and passion in their marriages, but they often feel their efforts are unsuccessful. So consistently romancing their wives seems too difficult, like trying to hit a constantly moving target. Some days they get lucky, but most of the time their efforts fall flat. So over time, they may quit trying or, at best, give romance only a half-hearted effort.

Obviously, some version of this frustration is true for women, too, even if the patterns might be different. Women often report their lives are anything but the romantic adventures they longed for when they were younger. The weight of too many responsibilities, the struggle to balance work and family, so many people to care for, no time for themselves without feeling like they're stealing something from someone they care about, and the never-ending daily routine—where's the romance in that?

The good news is that men and women were created for romance, passion, and adventure, and God wants each of us in the thick of it. He also wants us to feel fully alive and well cared for emotionally, spiritually, physically, and mentally (ESPM). Fortunately, He has empowered us with virtually everything we need to make it happen.

So what are we missing? Why is romance often so elusive and confusing? First, we need to examine some of the lies and misconceptions the media and our culture regularly thrust upon us. Candy, flowers, and expensive gifts may help fuel the economy, but they don't create lasting or satisfying romance. This is true no matter how much money we spend.

What about romantic environments? Imagine you and your spouse are at your favorite romantic location. Maybe it's sitting together in front of a roaring fire on a bearskin rug on a cold winter's night, sharing a glass of wine or a mug of hot cocoa. Maybe it's having dinner at your favorite restaurant with linen tablecloths, candlelight, and Vinny the violin player. Or perhaps it's taking a walk hand in hand on a moonlit beach on a warm summer's evening, with stars twinkling in the sky and waves lapping on the shore.

Do these environments create true romance?

No. Whatever the location or however expensive and beautiful the gift, not one of these things can create true romance. And here's why: If you take two people who have zero interest in each other and place them in that same perfectly romantic environment with lovely gifts and flowers, no romance will happen. However, if you take two people who *fascinate* each other and stick them in the middle of a Walmart parking lot on a drizzly, dreary evening, you'll see romantic sparks flying. *The essence of true romance is fascination and curiosity!*

That's why those moments of infatuation at the beginning of a romantic relationship are so compelling. In those moments, you find getting to know each other captivating. All you want to do is be together or talk on the phone as you discover new and amazing things about each other and dream about your possible future together.

Now, just because you can find romance in a parking lot doesn't mean that is where you should build your long-term relationship. Walmart probably won't be your favorite date spot in the future. Because if fascination and curiosity are present in your relationship and you include a special ambience with some well-selected gifts, you will surely fan the flames of passion and make them burn even brighter.

But fascination and curiosity can fade over time. For many couples, it can seem as if there is less and less to discover about each other. Things that made your relationship fascinating and adventurous lose their luster as life and routine become more of the norm. The relationship starts to feel like the same song played over and over. You once *loved* the song, but now it seems old and tired, like annoying elevator music or that looping tune you hear when you're on hold with customer service. *I've heard that song so many times, I'm kind of sick of it,* you tell yourself. *I want something new and exciting.*

Here's the good news: Boredom is entirely of our own making. There is realistically nothing *inherently* boring in this crazy world. To find someone or something boring, we must essentially turn off our natural curiosity. And that takes some effort. We were all born with a built-in fascination that makes us want to explore and touch everything (and for toddlers, stick everything in our mouths). There is always more to discover! We just need to stay curious, to keep looking for things that can be uncovered and unveiled. So keep investigating the new and the interesting. In the end, that discovery process is what keeps us feeling alive!

In marriage, no matter how much you think you already know about your spouse, there is always more to learn. Even though Jenni and I (Bob) have been married for more than forty-three years, I'm learning new things about her constantly. And just to keep things interesting, she keeps changing! She is growing and healing, learning more about God, and learning more about herself. But that's okay because I want the romance of discovery to last a lifetime, and I know that staying fascinated in getting to know her more over time is the key. I refuse to let boredom creep into our relationship.

I'm actually scared of boredom. When there's nothing new and exciting, I feel like a living dead person. Fortunately, one lifetime isn't close to enough time to fully get to know a human being, myself included. I've been living with *me* a lot longer than with Jenni, and I'm constantly learning new things about myself. *Is that new?* I sometimes wonder. *Have I always been that way?*

The opportunities to learn, grow, and discover are virtually endless, which is good news if you want your life and your marriage to be a romantic adventure of discovery. And if one lifetime isn't long enough to fully get to know any human, a hundred lifetimes aren't anywhere near enough time to fully get to know the Creator and Sustainer of the universe! If you want your faith to stay passionate, remain engaged in getting to know Him.

The recipe for really tapping into all the Lord has for you is to make your life and marriage a romantic and passionate adventure. First, let Him help you get to know yourself as He created you. Allow yourself to be truly interested, rather than viewing the process as a royal pain in the rear end. This will become a key component of a vibrant relationship with God as you allow Him to help you see yourself as He sees you. It is from this vantage point that you will become far more focused, energized, and effective in your pursuit of a life worth living and a marriage you and your spouse both enjoy. You will also discover a reason for living well that is worth the time and energy it actually requires.

My (Tara's) twenties were a challenging time for me. For a long time I didn't know who I was. My identity was unclear to me, and when an answer did come into view, I didn't like what I saw. I was single, and I regularly questioned what was wrong with me and why no one was interested in me. Slowly I began to recognize that my view of myself wasn't accurate. Over a time span of about six years, I began to explore who I was from God's perspective. I let go of my old perceptions and invested time and effort in getting to know Him and who *He* said I was.

I recall telling my sister about this change in my life. I said I felt I was slowly starting to like myself. She was thrilled for me, though a little saddened that I'd had such a dim view of myself before. Then a year later, we were talking again, and I made the same observation. She said she was a bit confused because I was repeating my previous comment. But for me, it wasn't confusing. It was a gradual journey. I was getting to know myself from God's perspective more and more every day. And there was so much to get to know!

I've allowed myself to enjoy this journey as I keep uncovering exciting things about myself that I've never seen before. After two more decades on this journey, I've learned to step into who God says I am. I continue to be curious and open with myself and others about who God created me to be. Rather than trying to be someone I was never intended to be, I've fully embraced this life-giving process of self-discovery.

We are always learning, growing, and healing, and it feels amazing when someone we love is genuinely interested in getting to know us, too, and wants to watch as the person we're becoming emerges. It feels equally amazing to marvel at what God is doing in our lives, even when our loved ones don't necessarily see it or acknowledge it.

Who Am I . . . Really?

Getting to know ourselves is an ongoing, lifelong investigation. There is always more to learn, and to keep things interesting, we all keep changing. We are always adjusting our approach to life as we move through an ever-changing world. Hopefully you will embrace this journey of self-discovery as an enduring portion of a good life as you allow God to be with you every step of the way. In time, this journey will become a regular part of your relationship with God as well as yourself.

The apostle Paul reminds us that "he who began a good work in you will bring it to completion at the day of Jesus Christ" (Philippians 1:6). God is the One at work in this journey. We partner with Him and surrender to what He is doing because He knows who we are better than we do. His perspective is always the correct one. When we really understand that, we can relax and enjoy the journey of growth and discovery with God to better appreciate what He has created.

Many therapists on the Hope Restored team use something we call the *Be List*. Cindy Irwin, one of our therapists, introduced this exercise to us. She developed it in her private counseling practice and found it to be a powerful way to help people explore their true identity. As she applied this technique, our team witnessed its impact and began to implement it in our own sessions. We'd like to offer it to you as a self-discovery tool.

This exercise helps you focus on a list of personal qualities and consider how they reveal your unique, God-given design.

Sadly, most people don't spend much time thinking about their positive qualities, but they do spend significant time dwelling on the negative. Yes, there can be value in attending to our struggles and shortcomings, but our negative qualities and behaviors are really just areas where we've lost sight of who God created us to be.

So we want you to focus on who you were created to be. That way you can intentionally work to make more of the real you what you and others experience and see. The exercise involves asking yourself to identify positive qualities about yourself in response to three questions:

1. What is true about you on your best day?
2. What can be true about you if you put effort toward it?
3. What qualities do you believe God wants to be true of you?

For the first question, write down six positive qualities you typically demonstrate. Use words that are more identity focused and descriptive of your character rather than various titles that may apply to you. (People often mix up what they do with who they are.) Here are some examples of identity-oriented qualities:

passionate	caring
adventurous	fun
understanding	seeking
bold	curious
patient	nurturing
meek	funny
kind	gentle
loving	faithful

honest	merciful
authentic	gracious
consistent	thankful
perseverant	welcoming
loyal	flexible
supportive	hospitable
visionary	confident
creative	
compassionate	fierce
disciplined	relaxed
empathetic	casual
warm	organized

Feel free to add other words to your list that more effectively describe you. After you've identified those words, draw a line underneath the last word and then come up with two qualities for the second question: "What can be true about you if you put effort toward it?" This question encourages you to think beyond the easily identifiable qualities that come to mind without much effort. These are qualities you currently possess but may need an additional push of positive intention to manifest.

Finally, for the third question—"What qualities do you believe God wants to be true of you?"—come up with at least one quality you know you possess down deep and feel that God wants you to develop. This question helps you consider the current leading edge of your personal growth and development.

Obviously, since we're all unique, everybody's list will look a little different. To more fully value and appreciate your individual differences as a married couple, it can be especially meaningful to place your two lists side by side. Once completed, your chart should look something like this:

Who Am I Designed to Be?

Husband's Design	Wife's Design
Fun loving	Loyal
Passionate	Hardworking
Devoted	Rambunctious
Creative	Caring
Sensitive	Generous
Open	Competitive
Adventurous	Thoughtful
Kind	Courageous
Courageous	Dependent on God

Remember, the purpose of this exercise is to help you gain a little clearer insight into who God created you to be, with the end goal of consistently *being* that person. Becoming who you truly are is actually the foundation of integrity. When we behave in ways that are contrary to who we really are, we're acting.

This Be List tool had a powerful impact on one of the couples I (Tara) interviewed. Mitchell and Anne shared about a conflict they'd had sometime after their marriage intensive, and how this tool changed their perceptions. Mitchell had always questioned his value, and as a result, he would consistently act out selfishly. After doing this exercise and embracing more of who he really was, he recognized his value and could hold on to that. He described it this way: "I keep going back to the value thing. I need to rest in the fact that I have value, that I don't need to let anything [cause] my sense of knowing I'm valued [to waver], and that I [can] continue to make value decisions. It would come out [in arguments]. She would say something, and I'd say, 'I'm not that person anymore,' and she'd say, 'I don't know that,' and I'd say, 'But I do.'"

Anne admitted that hearing him say that made her pause and remember the truth of who he really is at his core, and how God is growing and healing him. Because Mitchell embraced his Be List identity and learned to see himself as God does, he had the confidence and motivation to continue acting with integrity. His infidelity no longer defined him, and he could let those old behaviors go. He now has a much better knowledge of who he is and of God's unwavering love for him. As a result, he can behave in ways that are consistent with those truths.

Supercharging the Journey

I (Bob) had an unexpected encounter several years ago that surprised me. At the time, I wanted to love my wife better. I certainly loved Jenni and absolutely tried my best to love her well, but I felt that my flaws and mistakes were major obstacles. I knew I could do better. I just didn't know *how*. So I asked God for help.

As is usually the case in my relationship with Him, His response was to throw me a curveball. While it seemed He definitely wanted to help, I sensed Him asking me an unexpected question: *Bob, when you're speaking with Me, where do you imagine I am as we're talking?*

Immediately I pictured two places: either up in heaven sitting on His throne or right next to me like a trusted friend. *Why?* was all He said in response.

"I don't know," I replied aloud. "Where else would You be?"

Then He asked another (seemingly) off-the-wall question: *When you talk to children about accepting Jesus as their Lord and Savior, what do you normally tell them they need to do?*

I thought about it for a second and then promptly said, "Ask Jesus into their hearts."

He affirmed my response, then said, *So, Bob, is that where I live in you?*

"Yes, You do," I replied. I knew that Christ lived in me (Galatians 2:20). It was an important part of the Christian faith.

Then when you are speaking with Me, why do you imagine I'm in heaven or someplace outside your heart? Remember that I live within you, and every time you look at something, you can choose whose eyes you look through: yours or Mine.

All of a sudden, the significance of His words hit me like a ton of bricks. And then I saw an opportunity for something special and jumped on it. I asked the Lord, "Can You let me see Jenni through Your eyes?"

He didn't hesitate. *I'd be happy to.*

As I started looking at Jenni through these new eyes—through God's eyes—He showed me how He sees her. I noticed some things I'd never really seen before, but I also saw other traits of hers in a whole new way. As I began to compare my view with God's view, I got to choose which view I preferred. It's probably no surprise that I generally prefer His view!

God also showed me that I can actually experience His heart, which resides in me as well. As soon as I realized that, I asked Him, "Lord, can You let me feel what You feel for Jenni?"

Without hesitation, He responded, *I'd be delighted.*

And so I began to feel what He felt for her. This was amazing! Comparing my feelings with His, I knew that as much as I loved my wife, His love was far beyond mine.

As I practiced looking at Jenni through God's eyes and feeling what He feels for her, I experienced my love for her grow exponentially. This certainly turned out nicely for Jenni, but the benefits for me were unparalleled. I got to experience these amazing insights and feelings before she received anything from me! Why would I want any less?

But God had even more for me. One day I was in the bathroom, and I realized how much I hated mirrors. I spent as little time in front of the mirror as possible because I usually wasn't thrilled with what I saw staring back at me. But in that moment, I was reminded of my new eyes and my new heart toward Jenni. *Can I see myself that way?* I wondered.

With my subtle disdain for myself in mind, I asked God, "Can You let me see myself through Your eyes?"

His answer was the same: *Of course, My son.*

And then I asked, "Can You let me feel what You feel?"

He was delighted to again.

I began to see and feel for the first time just how much He loves me and how deep His desires are for me. Intellectually I already recognized this, but now I seemed to be *seeing* it and *experiencing* it live, in real time. And the contrast between my view and His was astounding.

So when I get to decide between my view or His and my feelings or His, guess which ones I choose?

This journey of learning more about myself and Jenni continues to this day. Why would I stop? In fact, it is so wonderful and powerful, I frequently ask God to let me see others through His eyes and feel His feelings for them. It changes what I see, how I feel, and how I behave toward them. When I do this, I always feel closer to being the man God created me to be.

Remember that God always reveals the *truth*, and sometimes the truth is less than beautiful. But if there are rough edges that need smoothing, or issues that need to be addressed and healed, keep in mind that these flaws represent thoughts, behaviors, or beliefs that are keeping us from God's best. He will meet us there, lovingly and patiently helping us heal and overcome. Why? Because He loves us too much to leave us stuck in that mess. He is always ready to deal whenever we're ready to meet Him there. No condemnation. No judgment. Simply deep, accepting love that sees the best in us and wants us to be able to live that out.

This simple, faith-based technique can help you more effectively tap into your omniscient (all-knowing) and omnipotent (all-powerful) Lord. As you consider embracing the journey of self-discovery, we hope you take advantage of this opportunity to see yourself through God's eyes and learn to feel with His heart.

Why Am I Here?

Part of our God-given design includes being created with a will that we are free to use as we choose. Yet as much power as we are capable of manifesting, we weren't given the power to make perfect choices. God designed us, and this world, to work in ways that are consistent with His purposes, and anything done apart from His will and design is destined to fail. We read in Scripture that "many are the plans in a person's heart, but it is the LORD's purpose that prevails" (Proverbs 19:21, NIV). Our best and most fulfilling plans will always involve living in harmony with God's design and finding our intended place in the unfolding of His plan and purpose.

When I (Tara) was in my midtwenties and was desperately seeking to understand my purpose and identity, I joined a small-group study on Henry Blackaby's classic book *Experiencing God*. One focus of that study stuck with me: Blackaby teaches us that as much as we might want to do great things for God in our lives, He is not necessarily *requiring* that of us. He may not have some bold new direction in mind for you. So when you are seeking God's direction, look for what you see Him already doing and join Him there. And if you're feeling lost or unsure about which way to go, go back to the last thing you felt certain God was asking of you and do that until you sense Him leading differently. It might be small and simple, perhaps focused on character building or personal growth. Do that first. God loves when we simply obey, even (and especially) in the small things.

Jesus taught, "One who is faithful in a very little is also faithful in much, and one who is dishonest in a very little is also dishonest in much" (Luke 16:10). We naturally are interested in the big potential purposes for our lives. But He wants devoted lives that He can lead in big and small ways. When it comes to following God's lead, I think we often feel like Daniel LaRusso in the movie *The Karate Kid*.[1] Mr. Miyagi's tedious instructions on how to wash a car or paint a fence initially confused Daniel. They seemed like such unimportant details! Wash this way. Paint that way. But practicing these muscle movements prepared Daniel for the bigger challenges he would face.

We don't always know what God is preparing us for, but He always has good purposes for us and our future. Sometimes following Him in the small things is what prepares us for the more significant events in our lives. Our job is to just follow His lead and trust Him the best we can.

The good news for God's Kingdom is that He will complete His plan with or without our participation. We may blow it, but God will accomplish His plan regardless. That truth is central to the hope of all Christians. *We know the end of the story.* The good guys win. But we must decide whether we want to be on the team and in the game or watching from the sidelines.

Remember, we have a free will, and our involvement in God's work is completely optional. This is true in both life and marriage. Is there any other way to live a life of genuine purpose than uncovering God's plan and then trying to fulfill it? Yes, we may have the freedom to search for alternative ways to find fulfillment, but we can't change God's mind, His plan, or any aspect of His design or purpose. So Bob and I always encourage couples to first try to discover what God is doing and then strive to find their place in it.

Sometimes we intersect with God's plan in our immediate, close-to-home lives; other times, we relate to our local communities, our nation, or the world. Occasionally, we might become part of something really big that attracts national or international attention. But more often, we engage in simple daily activities that people rarely notice.

But God notices. While He is certainly doing grand things around the world and throughout the universe, He is also interested in the lives of those we love every moment of every day. Any time we love someone God loves—when we invest in the lives of family and friends, strive to reflect His heart, and discover ways we can be a part of His plan and purpose—our lives have meaning. Apart from God, we have no life, and apart from Him, our lives have no eternal meaning or purpose.

‡

Prior to becoming a Christian in my early twenties, I (Bob) was the only lord I recognized in my life. It seemed quite clear to me that becoming a real man meant figuring out how to chart a life course that would lead to personal success and fulfillment. I had a deep sense that I could make a significant positive difference in the world, but I didn't know what that could be. It was all a big blur.

I had no connection to, or knowledge of, God's design or

plan. I did care about people—I saw a great deal of suffering around the world that troubled me—but since I had no real understanding of anything beyond this earthly life, my focus was simply on well-being from birth to death, achieving pleasure and success (for me and everyone else) with as little pain and suffering as possible. I had wonderfully high ideals, just no understanding of God's will.

When I became a believer, my perspective began to change. Suddenly the timeline I was referencing became much bigger. Human life is relatively short compared with eternity! Plus, I was no longer the lord of my life. I was serving a new Master, the One who created me, rescued me, and offered me the chance to be part of His grand plan, which has been unfolding since the beginning of time. Wow!

I began reading Scripture and hearing from the heart of God. I started interacting with others who loved and served Him. I experienced the Holy Spirit awakening my soul and my love for the Lord. I came to see His love for us and His deep desire to bring His goodness back to this world.

Then one day as I was reading in the Old Testament about King Saul's struggles, I came to the section where the prophet Samuel told Saul that his replacement (King David) would be "a man after [God's] own heart" (1 Samuel 13:14). Something about those words resonated deep within me, and I knew instantly that I, too, wanted to be a man after God's own heart. I wanted my heart and my life to reflect Him and His love.

That moment was a major course correction in my life. I wanted to know God and His will. I decided that I would strive to see what He was doing in the world and find my place within that plan. This journey of more than forty years has certainly not been without stops and starts, successes and failures. But I've always found my way back to that deep desire God placed within me to love others and serve my Savior.

What does it mean to be a person after God's own heart, to be fully empowered to love like Him? Perhaps you are well down that path already. Maybe you've developed many ways of connecting with the Lord and receiving guidance and direction. If what you're already doing is working great, don't stop. For everyone else, we want to offer some ideas that can guide you through the inexact process of trying to see where God is moving. These suggestions can help you discern His direction for you, how to get on board with what He is doing in the world, and how you can assume your place in His plan.

Of all the amazing Christian thinkers and mentors who have influenced us over the years, as well as the many excellent resources on discerning God's will, we have found the following advice most helpful.[2]

Don't Make Guidance Complicated

Your Lord lives within you and is always available. He wants to be close to you and speak into your life. Surrender your will to Him and let Him lead and guide you. That means letting His plans and desires be more important than yours. Our mortal enemy doesn't want us to draw near to God and follow Him, so be on the lookout for Satan's attempts to distract and confuse you. Remember that your Lord wants to guide your steps and use you for His purposes. He is always speaking to you and wants you to recognize His voice. Expect an answer when you call out to Him.

Pray for Guidance

Prayer is your primary way to communicate with your Lord. Even though He already knows your heart and mind, He desires an active relationship with you. That must include a two-way conversation.

God wants you to freely pour out your heart to Him, but He also wants you to listen. Listening to God is an essential aspect of effective prayer, but many people misunderstand this. Ask directly for His help and guidance; then quiet your heart and spirit and wait for Him to respond.

Read and Meditate on God's Word

The Lord can speak to you in many ways, but one of the most easily accessible ways to hear from Him is through reading and meditating on His Word. Meditating on Scripture is also an essential way to receive direction from Him. As you read, ask Him to speak directly to your heart and spirit through His Word. He can make it personal. If a direction you are considering conflicts with or is contrary to Scripture, it's a solid reason to pause and reconsider your course of action.

Allow God to Speak to You in the Way He Chooses

When seeking God's direction, be on the lookout for unexpected ways He may get your attention. There are no limits to the ways God can speak to us. Invite Him to speak to you in any way He chooses. Unusual "coincidences" are sometimes God in action. Prayerfully ask Him, *Is that You, God?* Also pray that He would clearly close the door and prevent you from moving forward if the direction you're considering is not of Him—or that He would open the door and allow you to proceed unhindered.

Seek Godly Counsel

You were given a powerful tool for navigating this life: your brain. Use it! God has equipped you with an ability to use good common sense and logic as you walk with Him. That includes seeking godly counsel from people who can help you hear from Him. But even the best counsel can be flawed and inconsistent with God's Word and His direction. So when you receive counsel from others, follow up with prayer, asking the Lord to either confirm their counsel or guide you differently. Never allow someone else's suggestions to take precedence over what the Lord is speaking to you as you pray and meditate on His Word. Keep in mind that you can be deceived and confused too. Allow the Lord to bring your spirit to a general peace with Him as He guides you.

Remove Any Obstacles to Hearing from God

Waiting for the Lord's guidance can seem frustrating at times because He works according to His timing, not ours. We may want an answer now, but He isn't beholden to our timetables. Trust Him and His timing rather than your emotional preferences.

Sometimes our ability to hear God can be obstructed by unconfessed sin. Like cotton stuffed in our ears, sin can make it difficult or impossible to hear from God. If you aren't hearing from Him, look inside to see if anything is blocking your ability to hear His voice so you can remove the obstacle by confessing any sin and receiving His forgiveness.

Practice Hearing God's Voice

Hearing from God clearly, effectively, and consistently is a skill we must learn. Like all skills, discerning God's voice takes practice. It is also developed through trial and error as we learn from our missteps and mistakes. The more you practice this skill, the better you'll get at it. The enemy wants to sit on your shoulder and whisper garbage into your ear. Learning to distinguish God's voice from other voices gets easier as you go. But be careful not to mistake your passionate desires for God's direction. Most of us unconsciously do our own God impressions, so take extra steps to make sure He is speaking, not you.

‡

As with everything we share in this book, the ultimate reason we do it is to help you develop a life-giving relationship with God. He doesn't need you—or any of us—to complete His plan. But apparently He doesn't want to do it without you. He desires your involvement for *your* sake, not His. He wants your life to be filled with rich meaning and purpose as you walk close to Him.

How great is that?

4

DISEMPOWERED
TO EMPOWERED

IN A WORLD THAT FEELS OUT OF CONTROL, we often find ourselves feeling powerless. From illness, famine, and death to injustice, crime, and violence, we're frequently reminded of just how powerless we humans are. Who doesn't want to feel a little empowered?

Feelings of powerlessness strike close to home in many ways. This is especially true in marriage. Many couples begin their marriages with beautiful hopes and dreams, only to end up struggling to make it work, falling into disillusionment, and finally giving up. As they watch their marriages slide into despair, love and hope slowly erode, and one day they realize their relationships are nothing like what they hoped for.

Theoretically, marriage is supposed to be different for Christians. We have great hope that our faith and our relationship with the

Creator of the universe will insulate us from the disappointments that nonbelievers experience. Shouldn't our marriages be better than non-Christian ones? Shouldn't we have advantages and opportunities as a result of our faith? Well, yes! Then why are so many marriages in the church struggling too? Shouldn't believers have greater ability and power to make our marriages the best they can be so they might satisfy the deepest longings of our hearts? The answer is a resounding yes!

God wants nothing but good things for His children, but we have our part to do too. We must learn how to use the resources He has given us. That doesn't mean we won't continue to experience difficulties, challenges, and hardships. We live in a messed-up, fallen world for now, and there is no escaping that reality. But God offers His children access to His unending resources to navigate the challenges of life and grow healthy relationships. He wants us to be fully equipped and fully empowered. As the apostle Paul expressed it,

> I pray that from his glorious, unlimited resources he will
> *empower* you with *inner strength* through his Spirit. Then
> Christ will make his home in your hearts as you trust in
> him. Your roots will grow down into God's love and keep
> you *strong*. And may you have the *power* to understand, as
> all God's people should, how wide, how long, how high, and
> how deep his love is. May you experience the love of Christ,
> though it is too great to understand fully. Then you will be
> made complete with all the fullness of life and *power* that
> comes from God.
> EPHESIANS 3:16-19, NLT (EMPHASIS ADDED)

As followers of Christ, we have been offered unique access to a source of power greater than our challenges here on earth. We see this truth throughout Scripture: God's love *empowers* us.

In this chapter, we'll explore how we can utilize this power by first looking at the ways we inadvertently disconnect from God, our power source. Then we'll investigate how we can more effectively plug into the power He wants to share with us. But first, let's take a moment to look at a central reality of God's intent and design.

No Life Apart from God

As human beings, we like trying to make it on our own. For many of us, our egos get in the way, and we proudly insist on being in charge of our lives. We believe this is proof of our independence, self-determination, and power. Some of us are quick to say, "I don't need you!" or "You're not the boss of me!" Others may simply be unaware that help is available.

Many Christians don't know how to connect deeply with God so they can benefit from His abundant love and resources. They don't realize how easy it is to inadvertently disconnect from Him. But the bottom line is that there is no life apart from God, and ultimately we cannot be successful in life or marriage without utilizing His love and power. Jesus declared,

> "I am the true vine, and my Father is the gardener. He cuts off every branch in me that bears no fruit, while every branch that does bear fruit he prunes so that it will be even more fruitful. You are already clean because of the word I have spoken to you. Remain in me, as I also remain in you. No branch can bear fruit by itself; it must remain in the vine. Neither can you bear fruit unless you remain in me.
>
> "I am the vine; you are the branches. If you remain in me and I in you, you will bear much fruit; *apart from me you can do nothing*. If you do not remain in me, you

are like a branch that is thrown away and withers; such branches are picked up, thrown into the fire and burned. If you remain in me and my words remain in you, ask whatever you wish, and it will be done for you. This is to my Father's glory, that you bear much fruit, showing yourselves to be my disciples.

"As the Father has loved me, so have I loved you. Now remain in my love. If you keep my commands, you will remain in my love, just as I have kept my Father's commands and remain in his love. I have told you this so that my joy may be in you and that your joy may be complete."

JOHN 15:1-11, NIV (EMPHASIS ADDED)

Here Jesus used an effective metaphor: He is the vine, and we are the branches connected to that vine. But then He said, "Apart from me you can do nothing." He didn't just mean that figuratively; He also meant it literally. There is no life apart from God! God's hand of sustaining grace is truly upon us. We would collapse on the floor dead without it. Apart from Him, we don't exist. This is true for all people, whether or not we recognize it.

We either operate under our own power, like a battery with a limited number of charges that eventually runs out of energy, or we stay plugged into the One who is our unending power source. His power makes life's challenges easier to overcome. Jesus says, "My yoke is easy, and my burden is light" (Matthew 11:30). And the apostle Paul reminds us, "I can do all things through him who strengthens me" (Philippians 4:13).

Living in God's power is much more fulfilling and effective than trying to live in our own limited power. It's how we were designed to live!

Giving Away Our Power through Blame

Blame is one of those protective reactions that humans naturally gravitate toward early in our development. It is also the second sin recorded after Adam and Eve gave in to the serpent's deception in the Garden of Eden. In Genesis 3, we read that when God asked them whether they had eaten of the tree He commanded them not to eat from, Adam blamed Eve, and then she blamed the serpent (verses 12-13). Neither of them owned up to what they did, nor did they repent. Have you ever noticed that? I wonder if God would have responded differently had either of them said, "You're right, God. I'm sorry."

Since humanity's fall, we've had a difficult time accepting responsibility for our sin and asking God to forgive us. We fear that if we own up to it, we'll have to live with the shame of what we've done—and that can seem unbearable. We believe the lie that finding someone or something else to blame can justify our actions and make us feel less guilty. Sadly, by blaming others, we bind ourselves to the shame and guilt we long to get out from under. Instead of experiencing freedom, we are prisoners of bitterness, resentment, and shame, which steal our joy and perspective. Hebrews 12:15 warns us, "See to it that no one fails to obtain the grace of God; that no 'root of bitterness' springs up and causes trouble, and by it many become defiled."

So how is blame so disempowering? I (Bob) learned this lesson in another humbling interaction with the Lord following several disagreements with Jenni. You see, when she did something that upset me, I believed that I should go to her and work it out, telling her what she did that I didn't like and what she could do differently. Seems reasonable, doesn't it? But for some strange reason, she never liked those conversations.

Please note that I also believed Jenni should approach me when *I* did something that bothered her. I don't think I handled those conversations well either, but I still maintained that they were the way to keep our relationship healthy and strong.

What's the problem with these sorts of conversations? The answer starts with understanding that many people dislike feeling powerless. It's certainly true for me—I hate those feelings. Few things in life make me more miserable. So when I spoke to Jenni one day about something she did that I didn't like and told her what she could change, she reacted, um, poorly. And then she stormed off. My immediate thought was, *How can we ever work through anything if she won't stay and discuss it?*

With Jenni gone, the only one I could complain to was God. And His reply woke me up! The questions I sensed Him asking me are questions I now regularly ask clients in therapy. As I share these questions, imagine He's talking with you when you've had a disagreement with your spouse.

In response to my protest about Jenni's disengagement, He asked, *Bob, right now, whom do you see as causing the problem?*

That was easy. "Well, Jenni for sure! Did You notice how she—"

God immediately interrupted with another question: *And whom do you see holding the key to a solution?*

Again, my immediate answer was "Jenni. If she would just stop disengaging, everything would be tons better."

His next question provided the conviction, insight, and opportunity I needed. *So, Bob, who has all the power here?*

"Jenni."

Then He asked, *And how did she get it?*

Wow! There was only one honest answer. If I viewed Jenni as fully responsible for causing *my* problem, and I believed she held the key to the solution, then I must have given that power to her.

God patiently and lovingly replied, *Bob, I didn't give you that power to give it away. I gave it to you to use responsibly and effectively to care for yourself well and then generously share your blessings with others.*

The exchange was eye-opening. I regularly felt as though Jenni held a lot of the power in our marriage, and I hated feeling powerless. But I genuinely thought that somehow she just *had* it. It had never dawned on me that I might be giving her my personal power! And for someone who dislikes feeling powerless as much as I do, it seemed really stupid. I saw that God was calling me to stop disempowering myself by blaming Jenni for how I felt or for holding control over my options. He was challenging me to accept that many things are beyond my control but my true power lies in how I respond to those situations and exercise my options within realistic limits. I also realized I have no righteous control over Jenni's behavior or the way she uses her God-given free will.

Sometimes we are victims of other people's choices, behaviors, or circumstances. But feeling and responding like victims is completely optional. We always have a choice to remember who we are called to be and how we will show up, regardless of what comes at us. On the Day of Judgment, that is the only thing we will have to give an account for.

As it turns out, the key to feeling more empowered has always been recognizing and embracing my personal responsibility. I've also discovered that I frequently add to the negative ways I feel in most situations. In fact, I've found that I often blame Jenni, and others, for things I have a significant, and unnoticed, part in. This is great news! If I'm causing some—or all—of my misery, I have the power to change it, and I don't need cooperation from anyone else to resolve the problem.

Codependency: Power in the Wrong Hands

Another way we give our power away is through codependency. *Codependency* is a good psychobabble term used to describe a situation in which we believe our ability to be fully who we were created to be—or feel what we long to feel—*depends* on someone else. We generally believe it goes both ways, too, so that the other person needs us in the same way. (Thus the term *codependent*.)

At times, human behavior can look and feel very controlling, while at other times, the ways we control situations are more subtle. But very often, we place responsibility into the wrong person's hands after expressing a need. It can sound like this: "If you don't do this or that, then I can't be okay." Or "I have legitimate needs here, and as my spouse, you need to meet them." Or even more subtle and romantic sounding, "You complete me."

Did you catch that? Somehow I can't be a whole person without you.

The overarching idea in codependent relationships is that aspects of *my* well-being are now *your* responsibility. Facets of this problem are reflected in comments like "I *need* you to love me in ways that are in line with my values and desires *so that* I can be okay and fulfill my God-given call." Or "I'll give you my heart, and you give me yours, and then we can both experience the fullness of marital bliss!"

These ideas sound romantic and perhaps even reasonable, and if you've bought into them, it's not really your fault. Our culture and the media sell this lie big-time.

Let's examine this problem. First, love is not about *need*. Deep and passionate love is always about *desire*! We don't *need* our spouses in order to live; we need God for that. We don't *need* our spouses so we can be fully who we were created to be. Again, that's between us and God. And we don't *need* our spouses so we can be fulfilled. God is our source. Now, this is not to say that our spouses can't make a major contribution to the quality of our lives. But Bob doesn't need Jenni in order to live or to be fully who he was created to be, or to be fulfilled. Nor does Tara need Vince in that way. We do, however, deeply and passionately *want* them. We are in no way dependent on our spouses, and we *can* live if living is without them (contrary to the old pop song). We just don't want to!

Second, as previously discussed, most problems in marriage are a result of misplaced responsibilities—either taking responsibility for things that aren't ours to take or *not* taking adequate responsibility for things that are. Each of us is fully responsible and accountable for our own well-being, whether or not we fulfill our life purpose. We also have a golden opportunity and privilege to contribute to our spouses' well-being, *but we aren't responsible for it*. Codependency gets all this confused and messed up, to everyone's detriment. Remaining crystal clear about who is responsible for what and doing *your* part but not your spouse's is critical to keeping your relationship healthy and running smoothly.

Couples often get wrapped up in needing or wanting their spouses to change. And while it's sometimes easy to agree that those changes would be in everyone's best interest, this fixation causes us to see ourselves as the Holy Spirit's self-appointed helpers in perfecting our spouses.

Our problem is having an incorrect understanding of what marriage should look like. We all enter marriage with certain expectations and values based on the culture, our families of origin, or even romantic fantasies of what constitutes marital bliss. The media and entertainment culture certainly contribute to this perspective. We have ideals in mind, and a little spousal adjustment could take us so much further, right?

The truth is that God intentionally created our spouses, and any attempt to change them places us at odds not only with them but with our Creator as well. Their personal growth and efforts to change are the sole responsibility of our spouses as, hopefully, the Lord directs them.

Elements of codependency can often show up subtly and unexpectedly. As mentioned earlier, I (Tara) married when I was thirty-one. I had also finished my master's degree in professional counseling, so I had a fair bit of education to influence how I expected and wanted my marriage to go. You may remember that I felt my husband and I would have significant challenges before things improved. But even with that knowledge, it was difficult to deal with our differences. One day very early in our marriage, after I had put the groceries away, Vince began reorganizing the fridge and cupboards so things were in their "proper" place. We had been adults for more than a decade and had our own ideas about these things.

I don't recall my initial reaction, although I suspect I was angry with Vince. You see, in reality, I not only wanted Vince to *behave* differently at the time; I also wanted him to *be* different. This was an emotional reaction, not a rational one, and boy was it strong! It was also an indication of some unrecognized codependency, as well as my powerlessness to change Vince. And it put me at odds with both Vince and his Maker. I was in a no-win situation, but I realized I had a choice: I could keep trying to get his attention and escalate the conflict so he would have to listen to me (that never works, by the way), or I could do something different that would restore my sense of empowerment.

Thankfully, I had already bought into the concept of taking personal responsibility for my well-being, and I ran to my Lord for help. I went to the bedroom and pulled out my journal. Even today I find that journaling is the best way to process my feelings when I am worked up. Writing helps me focus my thoughts and reconnect to God so I can hear from Him.

That day, I poured out all my complaints to the Lord in writing and asked if He was seeing all the things I was experiencing with Vince. I felt His loving presence with me, and I knew He understood.

Then, as I continued to pray and ask for perspective, I felt a gentle conviction and wrote in my journal what I sensed God saying to my spirit: *Tara, I know this is hard for you, and it is painful. Vince is My son, and I will grow him when and how I choose—that is not your business. I want you to be the wife I am calling you to be, regardless of how or if Vince shows up.*

Wow! That got my attention. I have never forgotten that gentle reprimand. You see, I believed that I couldn't have a happy marriage or be the wife I longed to be if Vince didn't get on board with all the good and helpful how-to tips I had learned. Thankfully, God redirected my focus to my own responsibilities, and together we began His renovation projects on my heart and life.

I'm not saying that the differences in how Vince and I approach life don't hurt sometimes, or that we don't hurt each other deeply on occasion. But I am saying that even when Vince hurts me and our differences are challenging, I don't have to force my way on him. I can return to God for comfort, loving reassurance, and a useful perspective change that helps me grow as He intends. I can surrender to His power and what *He* is doing rather than giving all my power away by focusing on what Vince is or isn't doing according to *my* design. As a result, I feel seen, loved, and empowered by God. The hurts of this world can't prevent me from receiving that.

Disempowered and Disconnected

If God created us to stay connected to Him and His power so that we can live our lives to the full, why don't we? Two primary culprits leading to feeling disempowered and disconnected are pain and fear. Both are unavoidable on this side of heaven, but when we understand what is actually happening within us, pain and fear don't have to be in control. Indeed, they can even lead us back to God and result in freedom and empowerment.

To help us get there, let's look under the hood and see why pain and fear so often trip us up. We are confident that this information can begin to pay immediate dividends, so bear with us through a brief bit of human biology. If you can't relate to some of the more extreme aspects of this content, you are likely in relationships with people who can.

Under the Hood

God wired our nervous systems to regulate and manage certain bodily functions automatically, without needing any awareness or decision-making on our part. These automatic functions include things like our heart rates, breathing, and digestion. But our nervous systems also manage our ability to perceive and react to danger, as well as to open up and connect with others when we feel safe. The challenge is that many of us have limited awareness of what is going on in our bodies, and as a result, we find ourselves at the mercy of shifting internal states. Most of us can recall situations when we either overreacted to something or shut down and then disconnected from the world around us in a way that seemed extreme given the circumstances. This can be quite disconcerting.

When our in-the-moment experiences feel more manageable, our ability to navigate life's challenges improves. We also have an easier time staying connected to God and can more confidently move in and out of connection with others.

First let's look at three key parts of the nervous system and the roles they play in our responses. Then we'll look at how, with God's help, we can gain more conscious control to better regulate our internal worlds. When we have more control over our reactions, we're much better equipped to improve all our relationships.

The first part of the nervous system we want to look at is the *parasympathetic nervous system.* This part of the nervous system sends calming messages to our bodies from a part of the brain called the *prefrontal cortex.* The prefrontal cortex is the conscious, thinking part of our brains that gives us access to logic, wisdom, perspective, impulse control, and response selection. It's also the last part of the brain to fully develop, even into our midtwenties. We like to think of it as the *mature, grounded adult part* of ourselves. When this part of our brains is online and engaged, it tells the parasympathetic nervous system to take over. In this state, we feel safe, relaxed, and calm enough to be playful, creative, curious, and even vulnerable. We also feel more connected to ourselves and more open to connecting with God and others. When our hearts are calm and open, connecting seems easy. We all love camping out here! God intended this grounded, peaceful, and mature part of ourselves to be in charge.

However, when a different part of our brains (the amygdala) senses that something is unsafe or upsetting, it knocks our grounded adult part offline and triggers another part of the nervous system, called the *sympathetic nervous system.* This is the second key part of the nervous system we'll focus on, specifically the part that comes online during infancy and early childhood.

First, let's look at the function of the sympathetic nervous system. This system is a protective mechanism that God created to keep us safe. This mechanism can trigger three different types of reactions in moments of danger: *the flight, fight, or freeze response.* When the brain picks up on something it perceives as a threat, it sends an alert signal to the sympathetic nervous system to prepare the body for action. Suddenly we feel a powerful surge of adrenaline. Our hearts speed up and pump more blood and oxygen to our muscles, our breathing becomes fast and shallow, our pupils dilate, and we may begin sweating. This isn't a conscious choice, and it can sometimes feel as if our nervous systems (or our intense emotions) have hijacked our brains. And in many ways, they have. The sympathetic nervous system serves the vital function of protecting us from perceived or actual threats. This natural process can also explain how we developed our less mature coping strategies, and why we can unconsciously return to them so quickly.

As babies and young children, we're not only small and helpless, but we also have limited resources to keep ourselves safe. Others need to care for us and protect us. When we're faced with a perceived threat, our only defenses are to shut down and submit in the face of danger when running away or fighting are *not* viable options. We call this the *wounded-child reaction.*

Perhaps you can relate to feeling as if the only way to protect yourself in certain situations is to shut down, and that fighting or fleeing would only make things worse. When your brain interprets the situation that way, your hijacked nervous system drops you into shutdown mode. Instead of feeling like a capable adult, you react as if you're a small, disempowered, and helpless little child again. Your energy plummets, and endorphins are released that help numb you or increase your pain threshold. In shutdown mode, you can consciously or unconsciously become disconnected from yourself, God, and other people. The doors to your heart slam shut. People pleasing or submission can seem like your only options to get out of the situation, and you can be left feeling unseen, unimportant, and lost. Remember, though, this is a God-designed system to help us initially cope and survive. We all have these moments, so try not to judge yourself if you recall feeling this way.

Unfortunately, if this part of our defense system is needed frequently during childhood, it can become a primary coping mechanism for us as adults, even when we have other resources to draw from. We may no longer need this extreme survival response, but if no one helps us understand what happened or shows us better alternatives, we can remain stuck in this cycle.

When some people feel threatened, they shut down emotionally and become numb and oblivious to what's happening inside them. Others who are more emotionally tuned in feel like frightened children. While the wounded-child reaction might be great for survival, if it's habitual, it can wreak havoc on our relationships. Since this coping strategy is largely unconscious, we can be completely oblivious to the negative impact it has on us or others.

This childlike defense mechanism can be seen in Anne and Mitchell's relationship from Tara's research. Both had dysfunctional and abusive childhoods. Mitchell often acted in selfish and childish ways without realizing he was shut down and largely unaware of what was really going on inside him and how his behaviors impacted others.

He described it this way: "I didn't fully understand that my choices impact [Anne], because every decision that was made around my life never took me into consideration, so why should I take other people into consideration when I make decisions? That's the way I lived because that's what I knew."

The third key part of the nervous system we want to focus on is the part of the sympathetic nervous system that comes online in later childhood and adolescence. By the time children become preteens and teenagers, they are physically bigger and stronger, and they have more options to keep themselves safe than infants and young children do. At this stage, instead of just shutting down, running away or physically defending themselves become options when they're faced with danger. Teens are bigger and stronger, but they still haven't reached mature adulthood, which provides additional resources. So teens may also engage in verbal outbursts and destructive, self-harming behaviors as they search for more control over their circumstances.

As with the wounded-child reaction, when the teen-like part of our brains is in control, we're no longer fully connected to ourselves or the world around us. We're in a reactive mode, and our adult brains are temporarily offline. We're on high alert, and our insides can feel jittery and chaotic. Our heart rates and blood pressure increase, and our bodies start pumping out neurochemicals like cortisol and adrenaline to energize us to either flee or fight. In these moments, we aren't exactly thinking logically, as the blood literally leaves our brains and moves to our extremities to prepare us to defend ourselves or run. We are still in survival mode, desperately trying to regain our sense of control and safety, but now we're reacting like slightly more powerful teens rather than frightened little kids. We call this the *protective-teen reaction.*

One helpful metaphor is to picture a car in an accident, with the engine on fire. When emergency services arrive, they do whatever is necessary to get the driver out of the car. Collateral damage doesn't matter in life-or-death situations. Teen emotions often feel that way. Everything is urgent and dire. When we're in the protective-teen mode, we are still reacting and generally not thinking carefully through the consequences of our words and actions. Only later, when we calm down and reengage the mature adult part of our brains, can we look back and evaluate what happened. Too often we feel regret or even shame because of our reactive behaviors.

To illustrate, let's look at another one of the couples Tara interviewed. Michelle and Kofi's arguments often got pretty toxic. Both were in fight mode trying to protect themselves from further hurt, but it didn't work. Their protective-teen modes were fully engaged.

Michelle described it this way: "[Kofi] would always attack my family. You know, he would go there—really, really vulnerable places that are really hard to heal. And I would emasculate him, you know, so we were equal offenders."

Unfortunately, Michelle and Kofi didn't make the changes they needed to, and during Tara's study, Michelle reported that they were in the process of divorcing. They let their fight responses dominate and were unwilling to take the time and energy needed to see what was really going on so they could move toward a more productive and relationship-enhancing adult mode.

The hard part about having nervous systems that are so reactive and automatic is that it's easy to interpret the world based on our childhood programming. So, as adults, we may consciously know we aren't in any real danger most of the time, but when our conditioned nervous-system responses get triggered, they have the power to knock the grounded adult part of our brains offline and take us back to either a protective-teen reaction or a wounded-child reaction. When we find ourselves stuck in either of these more reactive states, we end up feeling disconnected, disempowered, and dysregulated, and all our relationships suffer!

So how do you get your adult brain and your power back online when you're at the mercy of your unconscious automatic nervous system? Good news! With practice, you can begin to slow things down and notice when your wise, grounded adult brain has gone offline. The evidence is obvious once you pause long enough to see your protective knee-jerk maneuvering. Noticing what is going on, and even labeling it without judgment, is a beginning. You're feeling threatened and are trying to stay safe. That isn't inherently bad! The question is *Are your habitual responses really working? Are they helping you achieve your best results?* The shift in focus and increased awareness can help you make the unconscious conscious. Instead of letting simple knee-jerk reactions control you, bring your adult brain back into the equation. Conscious awareness allows you to begin intentionally looking for better options.

I (Tara) vividly remember shifting into protective-teen mode one afternoon when it felt as if Vince was disrespecting me. It didn't happen during an argument or anything distressing. He simply got distracted while I was talking and walked out the back door. In an instant I was furious! My heart was racing, and I couldn't think clearly. When he came back in, he was surprised to see me in such a state. I accused him of walking out while I was talking, and he said he thought I was finished. I fumed, "I was in the middle of a sentence!" And he quickly apologized, then left the room (maybe his flight response?).

I stood at my kitchen counter literally shaking. I began to notice my body reacting and took a few deep breaths. My adult brain started to come back online, and I became curious about my extreme fight reaction. (*Side note:* Curiosity helps us come back online, whereas judgment pushes us back down and keeps us spinning.) Such an extreme reaction is not typical for me. Without beating myself up, I committed to revisiting this experience when I wasn't in the middle of making dinner to see what was at the root of it. Then I began to gently soothe myself. (We'll talk about how to do this in chapter 6.) I also plugged into the Lord and reminded myself that God was with me, He saw me and what was happening, and He loved me. You might be surprised, but that message is extremely powerful in calming an activated nervous system.

EXERCISE

Simply remind yourself that God is with you, He sees you and what is happening, and He loves you. Focus on these truths in the moment. Take a few deep breaths as you allow these words to wash over you. You are okay at this moment. Notice how your body feels as you do this. Keep focusing on these reminders, breathing deeply, and noticing your body until things start to settle.

Connecting to Our Power Source

We have highlighted a few of the ways people find themselves disconnected from God. We would now like to give some practical suggestions for reconnecting with God and deepening that connection. Looking to Jesus as a model for staying connected to the Father is a great starting place. We also have a rich library of practices that Christ followers have applied to their faith for centuries. These classic spiritual disciplines—which many deep Christian thinkers, such as Richard Foster and Dallas Willard, have outlined and categorized—include prayer, meditation, fasting, study, simplicity, submission, solitude, service, confession, guidance, celebration, and worship.

These practices have long track records of helping people of faith enter God's presence, hear clearly from Him, and better tap into His guidance and empowerment. While these practices might seem simple, they aren't necessarily easy. They take effort and practice, which is why they're called *disciplines*.

You may find some of these disciplines easier to practice, and some may resonate more deeply in your relationship with God. Others may require more intentionality, and you'll discover the benefits as you actively develop your relationship with God. Some are inwardly focused, while others move you toward relationship with other Christians. Some are about letting stuff go, and others encourage additions to your journey.

Through these spiritual disciplines, we hope you'll experience God more intimately, learn to trust Him more fully, and become more open and receptive to Him.

Prayer

Communicating with God in prayer is the most obvious and common spiritual discipline. Although it can include your requests and petitions to God, prayer is more about learning to listen to Him and consider His thoughts and heart. Through prayer, you partner with God in what He is already doing, combining your thoughts and energy with His. The apostle Paul instructs us to "rejoice always, [and] pray without ceasing" (1 Thessalonians 5:16-17).

Pray without ceasing. How is that possible? Think of prayer as an ongoing, two-way conversation with the living God who walks beside you and lives within you through His Spirit. Prayer is far more than just talking, unless you think what *you* have to say is more important than what *He* has to say! Learn to keep your heart open to God's heart and your ears tuned in to His will as you go about your daily activities. Prayer is about practicing being aware of God's presence, which includes constantly listening for His voice. While there are many formal ways to pray, God loves our simple prayers too. He wants to walk with you and talk with you!

Meditation

This discipline is centered around sharpening your focus on God and His will, internalizing His truth, and allowing that truth to impact your decisions. Through meditation, you not only seek to know what God says, but you allow it to change you. Unlike Eastern meditation that invites you to *empty* your mind, Christian meditation is about *filling* your mind with the mind of Christ. It includes pondering God's words and allowing them to come alive within you. It is a way of seeking a more intimate relationship with God. Through this focused attention, you will find yourself loosening your grip on the things that distract you and compete for your attention, and filling yourself instead with a greater awareness of God's presence and love for you.

Fasting

Fasting means abstaining from food (not water) for a set period of time; however, it is materially different from a diet, which is limiting food or certain food categories for health reasons. As a spiritual discipline, fasting can serve several purposes, but the ultimate goal is to free up time and energy to more fully focus on God. Few activities in life consume more time, attention, and energy than preparing to eat and then eating what we prepare. Since feeding our bodies is essential for life, this makes sense. During a fast, that time becomes available to invest in spiritual endeavors like prayer, meditation, and other spiritual disciplines. Fasting can also reveal unconscious bondage to our eating habits. Often, we don't realize the hold these habits have in our lives until we choose to abstain from food for a time. This is true of physical and mental habits surrounding regular meals as well as snacks. The new awareness you gain from fasting can help you break free from food-related bondage. Fasting also provides opportunities to uncover issues in your life that may be obstructing or limiting your relationship with God.

Study

Studying God's Word is different from reading a devotional book. It's an investment of time and energy in getting to know God and His will through a deeper understanding of His Word. That is the ultimate purpose of study, reflected in the apostle Paul's words: "Do not be conformed to this world, but be transformed by the renewal of your mind, that by testing you may *discern* what is the will of God, what is good and acceptable and perfect" (Romans 12:2, emphasis added). If you aren't intimately familiar with God through studying His Word, your desires and opinions can easily lead you astray without your realizing it.

The primary focus of studying Scripture is learning what the text actually says, what it would have meant to the original audiences, and how it relates to the greater context of the book and the whole Bible. It can also include a slow, repetitive reading of a section of Scripture, looking at structure, noticing patterns, observing word choice, understanding the historical and cultural context, and exploring how scholars may have interpreted these passages. Other key aspects involve reflecting on what the message means for you today and applying it to your life.

Bible study isn't about blindly agreeing with what others say; it's about engaging your mind and wrestling with God's written Word to personally gain greater understanding.

Simplicity

In a world filled with busyness, information overload, noise, confusion, and more stuff than most people can manage, simplicity is often hard to find. Sadly, the frantic pace and complexity of life can keep us distracted and out of touch with ourselves, with others, and with God. In his book *Celebration of Discipline*, Richard Foster defined the discipline of simplicity as an "*inward* reality that results in an *outward* life-style."[1]

As you practice this spiritual discipline, focus first on simplifying your inner world by noticing ways in which you internally create complications and then seeking ways to create more inner space and breathing room. The second step is to simplify your outward life and activity.

Remember that reducing life's complexities is not the ultimate goal or purpose of simplicity. The purpose of simplicity is to free yourself to hear from God, to better connect with others, and to be less encumbered so you can respond to His leading.

Submission

Many people today view submission as giving in and giving up. Viewed this way, it can feel like defeat. As a spiritual discipline, however, submission provides an enormous opportunity to experience true freedom! We all have a God-given will and have been given the freedom to apply it as we choose. Unfortunately (or fortunately), we haven't been given the power necessary to make the world and everyone in it submit to our desires. If you're committed to getting your own way when things are beyond your control, it becomes a form of bondage. Nathan Foster shares that "submission is the spiritual discipline that frees us from the everlasting burden of always needing to get our own way. In submission we are learning to hold things lightly."[2]

In Ephesians, the apostle Paul encourages us to value others above ourselves, "submitting to one another out of reverence for Christ" (5:21). Included in submission is respecting and caring for ourselves by learning to embrace our human limits and living within them.

Solitude

By design, we are communal beings who are meant to live in active collaboration with other people. However, the discipline of solitude invites us to pull away from the busyness of life and find a quiet place to be alone with God. Solitude is a discipline in which we practice finding fulfillment in the presence of God, who never leaves us. It is a refocusing time that enables us to be open to God's leading rather than allowing the thoughts, opinions, or desires of others to pull us away from Him. Jesus regularly withdrew from other people to pray in solitary places (see, for example, Matthew 14:23). Silence is often paired with solitude in descriptions of spiritual disciplines because we also need to pull away from the noise and distractions of life.

Most people in our culture today have little to no experience of silence. Pulling away from the physical noise of your life, as well as learning to quiet the inner noise of your racing thoughts, will enable you to better tune in to God's often-quiet voice as He communicates with you. Solitude and silence are about learning to listen.

Service

The discipline of service involves noticing and seizing opportunities to assist and invest in others. Sometimes we serve in ways that others may notice and acknowledge, such as donating a large philanthropic gift or helping at a food bank. But most often, acts of service are behind the scenes, barely noticed and unacknowledged. Recognized or not, service is meant to be a response to God's initiative and prompting—a desire to serve the Lord out of gratitude for what He has done for you. If your desire is to receive acknowledgment and accolades from people instead of an affirming nod from your Father in heaven, your motives are likely suspect. Serving is your chance to join with God in His work in even the smallest ways. Ideally, it will become as natural to you as breathing.

Wonderfully, God is in the business of continually blessing His children. Yet as much as He desires to bless us, the benefits of His gifts are never meant to end with us. God promised Abraham, "I will bless you and make your name great, so that you will be a blessing" (Genesis 12:2). God reveals His heart when He says that we are blessed to be a blessing. In other words, He wants each of us to receive His generous gifts, allow them to fill us, and then look for ways to share those blessings and invest in others.

Confession

Sin is like cancer, and unconfessed sin can eat you alive, creating a major barrier in your relationship with the Lord. The discipline of confession provides a way to keep the pathways between you and the Lord clear, allowing you to receive God's forgiveness, healing, and freedom. Our Lord is light and lives in the light (1 John 1:5, 7). Satan, our mortal enemy, preys in the dark, hidden places. When we sin, we're usually embarrassed and ashamed of acting in ways that are contrary to who we were created to be as reflections of our Lord. Shame typically causes us to hide our sin, creating a pocket of darkness in our hearts. This is where Satan operates, and it's one of his favorite ways to capture us.

When we keep our transgressions hidden, we relegate ourselves to bondage. But when we confess our sin, we bring it out of the darkness into the light, which effectively neutralizes its hold on us. This dynamic is beautifully articulated in 1 John 1:9: "If we confess our sins, he is faithful and just to forgive us our sins and to cleanse us from all unrighteousness." Confession restores unhindered fellowship with our Father.

Guidance

The discipline of guidance is a spiritual practice of learning to hear God's voice, receive His direction, and respond as He leads. As we mentioned earlier, each of us was created on purpose with a purpose. Wise humans understand that we are limited by design and were not created to successfully make it on our own. As you surrender your life to God, allowing Him to empower you and direct your steps, you position yourself to access the only reliable source of life leadership. (We'll provide more details about this important discipline in the next chapter.)

Celebration

Life is a gift from God, and from the moment He conceived you in His mind, His intent was for you to live with Him forever. This fact is cause for daily joyful celebration, "for the joy of the LORD is your strength" (Nehemiah 8:10).

The discipline of celebration involves learning to shift your perspective to God's goodness regardless of your circumstances. Even when distressing or terrible things happen in your life, remember that God is always with you. As followers of Christ, we don't rejoice in evil when it seems to prevail. We rejoice in knowing that despite all the evil and ugliness around us, the One who lives within us will rescue us in the end, and He will prevail.

Each day, ask the Lord to show you His goodness in all things, then give thanks for His provision. As you practice the discipline of celebration, His joy will become your joy. Your loving Father delights to hear you laugh and see you play. When others see your deep joy, even in the face of less-than-ideal circumstances, you become a beacon of light and hope in a world that often looks hopeless.

Worship

As we celebrate our incomprehensibly benevolent Lord and Maker with deep gratitude and profound reverence, a yearning to proclaim His goodness wells up within us. We enter the discipline of worship when we declare, shout, sing, or merely bask in that reality. In its purest form, worship is a response to a blessed touch from our loving God in the deepest parts of our being. Richard Foster describes true worship as "the human response to the divine initiative."[3] This is commonly expressed through songs and words of praise. Worship is an intensely personal experience but has some of its most meaningful expressions when we join together as a corporate body of believers. Beyond the personal benefits, worship as a community is a tremendous source of encouragement. So "let us consider how to stir up one another to love and good works, not neglecting to meet together, as is the habit of some, but encouraging one another, and all the more as you see the Day drawing near" (Hebrews 10:24-25).

‡

If you're interested in practicing some of these spiritual disciplines in your private time with God, give the exercises in appendix A a try.

God Wants to Empower You!

Instead of remaining stuck in old patterns and a dysregulated nervous system, you can tap into the power God desires to give you. His power is continuously available if only you'll turn to Him and ask.

He wants to empower you through His immeasurable love!

When that love takes root in your heart, you will become complete in Him, filled with His power. And as you trust Him and His love for you, He will enable you to see things from His perspective.

There are many ways you can actively cultivate an intimate relationship with God, though at times it may mean letting go of *your* ways altogether. However, He promises that when you do, He will not only empower you, but He will also fill you with surpassing peace, joy, and freedom

Keep the door to your heart open to receive God's love and live in continual connection with Him. Few things are more effective at positioning you to build a dynamic marriage and be a great spouse!

5

THE SECRET DOOR
THROUGH CONFLICT
TO EMPOWERMENT

SO FAR, WE'VE FOCUSED ON LEARNING how to claim our true identity in Christ, fulfill our reason for being, remain plugged into God as our power source, and join with Him in His work. Next we'll talk about one of the most common reasons people get seriously stuck in marriage: *conflict*.

Every relationship experiences conflict, and the more important the relationship is, the worse the disagreements seem to be. We all invest more in relationships that are important to us, so we have more to lose. And since husbands and wives are not only fundamentally different from each other but also possess irritating free will, our differences *will* clash. Conflict in marriage is virtually unavoidable.

But there's good news too! And it starts with recognizing that the problem on the surface is seldom the *real* problem. What we initially see as the reason for our conflict is often some smaller issue we disagree on. But we add to that problem, inflating our perception of the issue by directing our attention to any number of our spouses' unfortunate behaviors. And we start to think those behaviors caused the issue or are making it worse. So that blasted first issue (whatever it is) is a real stinker, but then our spouses keep acting in ways we don't like as well. Yet all these problems are on the surface.

Underlying every human conflict is a predictable pattern, and if we look below the surface to see what is *really* driving those conflicts, opportunities emerge to be empowered in ways we never would have anticipated.

Blame is disempowering, and focusing on our spouses generally gets us nowhere profitable! So as we unpack the realities of marital conflict together, focus on what *you* are responsible for and where *your* real power lies. Fix your attention on your side of the relational equation. This is not to suggest that what your spouse is doing doesn't matter. It certainly does! But you have no power or responsibility there.

By shining the spotlight on yourself instead of your spouse, you'll begin to see the things that are keeping you from being empowered. Understanding yourself better and exploring your side of a conflict can often reveal what is driving your behaviors, habits, and strategies. Your weaknesses, insecurities, unresolved pain, and personal limitations are often your greatest opportunities to heal and grow—and to enjoy being your best self.

Of course, no one ever wants to focus on their limitations. We're rarely motivated to lean into the rigors of the work required for personal growth and healing, especially if life seems to be going pretty well. The work is hard and uncomfortable, and we just want to enjoy the good times as long as possible. But conflict with someone we love usually feels crummy, and we want to quickly get to a better place. That's what motivates us to do the work required to heal and grow.

"GOD IS . . ."

It's worth taking a moment to remember some important truths about who God really is, so you can trust His goodness and commitment to your well-being and relax in Him through the self-discovery process. Consider these well-known words from the love chapter in 1 Corinthians 13: "Love is patient, love is kind. It does not envy, it does not boast, it is not proud. It does not dishonor others, it is not self-seeking, it is not easily angered, it keeps no record of wrongs. Love does not delight in evil but rejoices with the truth. It always protects, always trusts, always hopes, always perseveres. Love never fails" (verses 4-8, NIV). What a beautiful description of love!

But when you consider that "God *is* love" (1 John 4:8, emphasis added), what you have now is an amazing description of our Father in heaven. We like to read 1 Corinthians 13 this way: "God is patient, God is kind. He does not envy, He does not boast, He is not proud. He does not dishonor others, He is not self-seeking, He is not easily angered, He keeps no record of wrongs. God does not delight in evil but rejoices with the truth. He always protects, always trusts, always hopes, always perseveres. God never fails."

That's who wants to walk with you and guide you down the pathway He intended for your healing, freedom, peace, and power!

The Reactive Cycle

Have you ever noticed that during conflicts with your spouse that the things you argue about might be different but the resulting feelings are similar? It's as if you're returning to a place you've been before. You might also notice that while you're fussing about the little things, you're missing something truly important: The rocket fuel that is driving your responses to each other is where the power to change things for the better actually lies. We call this consistent and predictable pattern the *Reactive Cycle*.

Over the years, we have developed an effective tool to map out how this destructive cycle works in marriage and how to break it. In this chapter, we'll provide a short description that will enable you to map out your own reactive cycle so you can see how it works. (For an in-depth exploration of this cycle, we recommend the book *9 Lies That Will Destroy Your Marriage*.)

Buttons and Reactions

When mapping out your own reactive cycle, there are three steps you'll need to follow. The first step is to identify *the feelings that get triggered* when conflict happens in your marriage. These are your *buttons*. To help you identify your feelings, read through the "Feeling Words" list in appendix B and put a check mark next to words that describe the way you've felt in conflicts with your spouse. Next, review the words you checked and put a star next to your top five. These stars represent your buttons, the most common or intense feelings you experience in conflicts.

The second step is to identify *typical reactions* you experience during conflicts with your spouse. Read through the second list of feeling words in appendix B and put a check mark next to words that describe how you've reacted when you're engaged in a conflict.

Then put a star next to your top five. These stars reflect your most common, favorite, or intense reactions.

The third step is to identify *the good things you desire in your marriage*. Read through the third list in appendix B and check all the words that describe what you desire in your marriage. Then put a star next to your top five. (These can be things you are already enjoying.)

After completing these steps, write your top five buttons, your top five reactions, and your top five desires in the corresponding sections of the empty Reactive Cycle map in appendix B. Here is an example of what Tara and Vince's reactive cycle looks like:

Tara's Wants
wanted
understood
adequate
affection
companionship

Vince's Buttons
failure
disappointment
helpless/powerless
not good enough
misunderstood

Vince's Wants
appreciation
assistance
comfort
companionship

Reactive Cycle

Tara's Reactions
anger
defensiveness
independence
negative body language
criticize

Tara's Buttons
controlled
rejected
insignificant
judged
misunderstood

Vince's Reactions
avoidance
control
pessimism
shut-down
blame

What's interesting about this map is how each component oddly and consistently interacts with other components. We can't exactly explain why this is so common and predictable for everyone, but it is. When one spouse's button is pushed, they will naturally react because they don't like how it feels. Their reaction will push one of their partner's buttons, and spouse number two will react because they don't like their own newly triggered feeling. Spouse number one probably wasn't trying to upset their partner, but they did nonetheless. When spouse number two reacts, that will likely press a button in spouse number one, who will, of course, react. This presses *another* button in spouse number two, and then they're off to the races! This is the Reactive Cycle, and we all follow it.

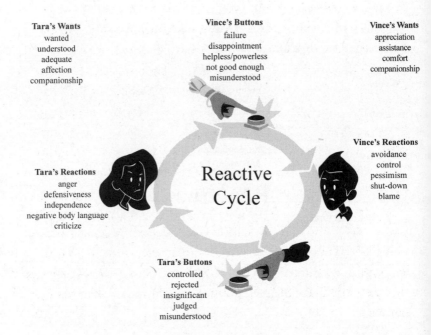

Tara's Wants
wanted
understood
adequate
affection
companionship

Vince's Buttons
failure
disappointment
helpless/powerless
not good enough
misunderstood

Vince's Wants
appreciation
assistance
comfort
companionship

Vince's Reactions
avoidance
control
pessimism
shut-down
blame

Tara's Reactions
anger
defensiveness
independence
negative body language
criticize

Reactive Cycle

Tara's Buttons
controlled
rejected
insignificant
judged
misunderstood

How This Works in Everyday Life

Let's look at a simple example in our (Tara and Vince's) marriage to see how the Reactive Cycle spins. On a recent vacation, Vince was triggered when a waiter got our order wrong. We intended to get a starter and a main dish, both to share. Rather than sharing one meal, the waiter brought two separate orders. We thought he had simply divided the order into two plates but when the bill came, we were charged for two full orders. Because precision is so important to Vince and this ended up costing us more money, his "disappointment" button got pushed. He hates that feeling! He reacted by blaming me because I had placed the order. I immediately felt judged and reacted in a defensive way. This further triggered Vince, and he reacted. I felt rejected and started to more openly criticize him. Internally, I began to stew in negative thinking about him and our marriage.

This type of conflict can go on for quite a while and frequently ends with both spouses feeling miserable and distant. You see, we naturally focus on our spouses' reactions and how wrong or bad they are. In reality, though, the underlying problem is not our reactions, even though they are always unhelpful and will never help us get what we want. No, the real heart of the cycle—the rocket fuel that propels the entire thing—is the trigger, or button, that initiates a reaction. But triggers are rarely noticed, let alone attended to in any meaningful way.

As adults, we are 100 percent personally responsible for our triggers, fears, and buttons. When we attend to them, our perspectives change, and God empowers us to see the situation, ourselves, and our spouses in a new light. This allows us to behave in ways that are more likely to bring positive, powerful developments in our marriages.

Shadow Monsters and Hedgehogs

You may notice that Vince's and my (Tara's) reactions listed in our Reactive Cycle example generally fit into three categories: fight, flight, or shutdown. Sound familiar? Our reactions are almost always attempts to manage our feelings about some perceived threat. The degree of that feeling of being threatened varies, but it's always part of the cycle.

In the previous chapter, we discussed three ways our nervous systems react: like a wounded child, a protective teen, or a mature and grounded adult. We can see the first two reactions at play in the Reactive Cycle. What makes this so challenging is that most people don't realize that when they're triggered, their adult brains go offline, and their wounded-child or protective-teen reaction kicks in. This can happen in the blink of an eye and generally feels like a knee-jerk response. Because our nervous systems are constantly scanning for danger, we are kicked out of our adult brains before our conscious minds are aware of what's happening. When we feel threatened, fear is triggered, a button is pushed, and we instantly find ourselves in survival mode. This obviously doesn't result in a rational, patient response. In hindsight, it often looks like a seriously irrational overreaction.

Another thing that happens during the Reactive Cycle is that our internal critic, which we all have, tries to whip us into shape before outsiders can level their criticism at us. We may subconsciously believe that if we criticize ourselves first, the criticism of others won't hurt as badly. This can often be how we felt as children. Since we've already anticipated the criticism, we just tell ourselves the same things before others get the chance.

Knee-jerk reactions and self-criticism are coping strategies we develop as children or teens, and by the time we're adults they've basically become automatic. As we know, teen logic isn't ideal in adult situations, but our coping strategies worked before, so we repeat them until they become habits.

Immature coping strategies never contribute positively to adult relationships, and ultimately, they won't help us feel better. Sometimes we can find ourselves reacting more like a wounded child, shutting down to numb the pain or trying to make the danger go away by people pleasing or caretaking. These strategies don't work because one of them ignores what we really need, and the other attempts to manipulate people to stop our pain. In either case, the wounded child remains uncared for.

One thing these immature coping strategies do offer is a learning opportunity. If a mature adult provides us with a *positive* outside influence, practical instruction, and insightful guidance, we can develop healthier responses to conflict. In an ideal world, this is how the maturation process is supposed to happen.

If you didn't get this sort of guidance as a child, you now have the opportunity to learn healthier strategies with God's help. What you really need is to get your adult brain back online and in charge so you can develop more mature ways of responding to conflict. But it doesn't come easy. When your childlike or protective-teen reactions take over, your spouse likely won't see the hurting and vulnerable parts inside you that are desperately trying to get back to safety, connection, and well-being. They will see only the external reactions—and those reactions can look pretty hostile. We like to call them *shadow monsters* because they appear threatening.

As a kid, did you ever hold up a light to your hands and make silhouettes of creatures that cast shadows on the wall? Or maybe *you* were the monster, with a flashlight facing you and a huge version of yourself projecting onto the wall behind you. This was a fun game when we were children, but the adult version we're dealing with here isn't nearly as enjoyable. When our childlike emotional parts feel scared and vulnerable, they cast scary-looking shadows so they appear bigger and stronger and distract others from seeing that they don't feel safe or powerful enough to handle the threat. These shadow monsters are often what our reactions in our reactive cycles represent.

Shadow monsters may seem easy to recognize because the reactions are loud, intense, and overtly threatening, or at least actively seeking to engage in conflict. But for some people, flight mode or shutdown mode is a more common defense strategy. When threatened, they react by moving away, avoiding, distancing, or shutting down. We call this reaction the *hedgehog*. It's a bit like curling up in a ball of prickly quills that sting if touched.

It may appear less dangerous to an outside observer, but for a spouse, the hedgehog can feel just as threatening and distressing as the shadow monster, and it can make connection seem impossible.

While shadow-monster and hedgehog reactions may be effective in warding off danger, neither is effective in creating an intimate connection. It's possible to stay grounded and have compassion when we encounter our spouses' shadow monsters or hedgehogs, but it's difficult because we are also wired to protect ourselves (hence the Reactive *Cycle*). Often, the best move for all concerned is simply to retreat and give the shadow monster or the hedgehog time and space to let their adult brain reengage.

This reactive dynamic can take on an unfortunate layer of complexity when one spouse is carrying some large or small degree of unresolved trauma. The pain from past events becomes a filter through which that spouse views and interprets the other spouse's behavior and reactions. When conflict arises, spouse number one may project their own shadow monster or hedgehog onto spouse number two, imagining a level of threat that may not be there. As spouse number one looks at their partner through the eyes of their own shadow monster, they see only more monsters, even when their spouse is not behaving as badly as their nervous system perceives. This can be painful and confusing because, from a place of unresolved trauma, what spouse number one perceives seems completely real and reliable. They aren't aware that they're looking through a trauma lens rather than seeing present-day reality.

Julie, from Tara's research, was able to catch one of her mistaken perceptions that had often made her feel worse about her marriage and her life. "No one's intentionally sitting around trying to be mean to me, which is what I used to think," she reported. "It's just how life is, and if I can take care of myself, then I'm better."

This new insight came after she became aware of her habitual knee-jerk reaction to a trigger. She was able to see how quickly she unconsciously projected her fear onto her husband, David.

This helped her step back and look at the situation differently. Her shadow-monster projections disappeared when she turned on the lights to see what was true.

One way to catch knee-jerk reactions is to notice when your reaction seems bigger or more extreme than the situation warrants. This generally requires you to pause, step back emotionally, and try to observe yourself and the situation more objectively. Another clue can be when you detect your reactions regressing and you feel more like a powerless child than a full-grown adult.

Most people overreact or regress on occasion, sometimes more intensely than at other times. In the next chapter, we will share some basic ideas and practical tools to help you explore self-care as you begin or enhance your healing journey.

If these challenges and our solutions seem too overwhelming or complex to work through on your own, reach out to a professional therapist for help. There is no shame in needing a little extra help from time to time. Sometimes we just need the perspective of a skilled and objective person. You are worth it! You are God's child, and He is on this journey with you.

In the previous chapter, I (Tara) shared an experience about my protective inner teen hijacking my adult brain when Vince walked away while we were talking. At that moment, I wasn't able to explore what had set me off so strongly, but I recognized my reaction was way out of proportion. Vince couldn't see my hurting inner parts behind the big, angry shadow monster I was projecting. And naturally, when he encountered my scary projection, he fled (a classic hedgehog maneuver).

After spending some time exploring which of my buttons Vince may have pushed, I discovered that my reaction must have tapped into something big from my past. From a number of circumstances earlier in my life, I now have a hot-wired button anytime I feel overlooked or set aside. Vince's action pushed that button, and my brain interpreted the event as evidence that I wasn't worth his attention. Vince wasn't trying to do that at all. Perhaps he'd been a little careless with my heart, but I'm certain it was an unintentional distraction on his part. Nonetheless, we both got to see my shadow monster for a few minutes. It's never pleasant, but we all get our buttons pushed from time to time, and we react!

Breaking the Reactive Cycle

With the Reactive Cycle now in clear view and common coping reactions outlined, we want to show you how to stop the cycle dead in its tracks. Self-care is a big part of breaking this cycle, as we'll discover in the next chapter. But we must make a distinction between different kinds of self-care and how they relate to the Reactive Cycle. When we mention that people should take care of themselves, the first thing that typically comes to mind is what we call *proactive self-care*. These are the things we hopefully do every day to ensure that we stay healthy. Proactive self-care is just regular personal maintenance—getting adequate sleep, eating well, exercising regularly, and trying to maintain balance in our busy lives.

Interestingly, people rarely seek therapists for help with proactive self-care or to maintain good health. But the area where couples frequently need help is with *reactive self-care*. In other words, what do you do when your buttons get pushed and you feel triggered or upset? How do you take good care of yourself then?

Obviously, you need to care well for yourself in this area too! In fact, when your buttons get pushed, this is likely when you feel most in need of good self-care. Sadly, it's also an area where most people feel they fail the most.

When our buttons get pushed and we get upset, the worst parts of ourselves often come out—shadow monsters, hedgehogs, and any other creative defense mechanism we can muster—often come out. We commonly react in ways we regret afterward.

The hard part is that so often something the other person did really seemed wrong, bad, insensitive, or hurtful at the time. In fact, it really might have been. But if your response is unChristlike and unrighteous, it doesn't matter how bad your spouse's behavior is. You are still guilty. And if you become controlling, manipulative, angry, passive-aggressive, or pouty, you add the unfortunate consequence of becoming a person you don't want to be. But these characteristics are always contrary to who God created you to be. Thus, your behavior is the opposite of integrity!

To make matters worse, you are allowing your spouse's behavior to determine your own. In some very real ways, as we now know, you are giving your spouse power over you. When they act, you react as if you have no control. Thus, your common knee-jerk reactions are frequently a lose-lose-lose for you. You react in unrighteous ways, you become a person you don't want to be, and you give away your personal responsibility and power. Nothing about it feels like self-care, and you are caught in a miserable, and familiar, reactive cycle.

What can you do in those challenging moments? Where is your true power, and how can you take good care of yourself? The first essential step is to wake up and recognize that you have been triggered. You're in a reactive cycle, and you're heading down a path toward a miserable outcome for everyone. You must stop the cycle! But how do you do that when your spouse is being so difficult and keeps pushing your buttons? How do you, as an empowered individual, stop the cycle?

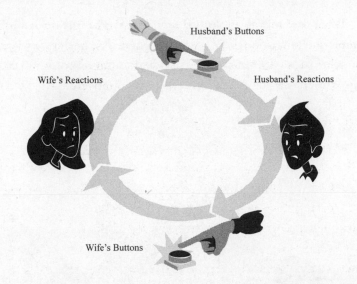

Husband's Buttons

Wife's Reactions

Husband's Reactions

Wife's Buttons

Well, where will your natural focus be directed when your spouse pushes one of your buttons? On what your spouse did, right? Obviously! But how much righteous control or power do you have over your spouse's God-given free will? Absolutely none!

When one spouse's buttons are pushed, where will they focus their attention?

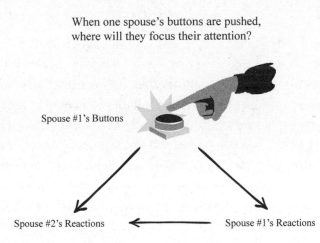

Spouse #1's Buttons

Spouse #2's Reactions ⟵ Spouse #1's Reactions

What can you do to stop the madness? The answer is both simple and powerful. That is not to suggest it's easy. The key is to create a space between your button and your reaction. In other words, exercise enough self-control so you don't react!

Stop the Madness
Don't react! Take full responsibility
for how you feel, what you do, and what you want and need.

You see, if the Reactive Cycle is spinning, it's a guarantee that you and your spouse are participating. Just like in a tug-of-war, the only way the game continues is if both of you keep pulling. If either drops the rope . . . it's game over. The same is true for the Reactive Cycle. If either of you can exercise enough self-control not to react, the cycle immediately stops. Sometimes it can feel as if it requires superhuman strength to control a knee-jerk reaction, but in the end, it's amazing how powerful self-control can feel. In fact, the personal and relational benefits are so great, self-control can become downright addicting!

Now, just because you stop the cycle doesn't mean that your spouse will. I (Bob) have had many arguments with Jenni when she wasn't even there. I said my lines, then added hers in my head and got angry at what she said because I knew that if she'd been there, that's what she would have said. But the Reactive Cycle wasn't actually going on between us anymore. Not reacting breaks the cycle.

However, as important as stopping the cycle is, you need to take it one step further. Merely shutting down, withdrawing, or avoiding doesn't actually get you or your relationship to a better place, even if it does stop the overt madness. Remember, hedgehogs stop, too, but the madness continues to spin.

What you insert in the space between your button being pushed and your reaction is what determines whether anything moves forward and improves. Instead of reacting, you can pause, refocus, and actually figure out how to care for yourself. This includes noticing what button was pushed, what you more deeply want or need, and what you can personally do to make sure you end up well cared for. Thus, you become less controlled by your circumstances and your spouse's behaviors and more able to come back to the relationship full, whole, and healthy as the person you want to be.

This is what I (Tara) did after Vince walked out in the middle of our conversation and I felt triggered. As soon as I realized we were in a reactive cycle, I took time to reflect, notice my triggers, and care for them. As I became aware of what was happening inside me, the internal reactive cycle I was engaging in, and the outward one I was engaging in with Vince, I slowly shifted my focus to caring for my heart and stopped focusing on Vince and his reactions.

In this case, thankfully, I sensed the Holy Spirit tapping me on the shoulder and drawing my attention back to my own yard.

He quietly and gently convicted me: *Is what you are telling yourself helpful, or are you making this worse?* Turns out those things I was telling myself about being less worthy and lovable were definitely making things worse—probably for both of us! Finally I remembered how to break this unpleasant pattern. I paused for a moment, shifted my focus from Vince and our reactive cycle to my inner self, and created space to care for my heart.

If you can pause the conflict with your spouse long enough to examine your reactive cycle and care for your hurts and fears, you can ultimately reclaim your power and bring your best self back to your spouse. You'll also have a far better chance of resolving the issue that started your conflict. No guarantees, but you greatly increase the odds.

Now let's focus on how to care for ourselves proactively and reactively.

6

WHAT DOES GOOD
SELF-CARE LOOK LIKE?

WE'VE NOW SPENT SIGNIFICANT TIME establishing the importance of taking personal responsibility so we can become fully empowered to love. For that objective to be accomplished, learning to care well for yourself is essential. Over time this must include establishing a life-giving connection to God as your Lord and Master, getting to know the real you as He created you, and understanding the direction He has for you in the Kingdom. Striving to be full, whole, and healthy is the only way to honor God's mandate and design for you, to care well for others, and to fulfill your intended Kingdom purpose. With a full reservoir, you will be equipped and empowered to share your resources with your spouse and others.

In this chapter, we will offer some tangible self-care ideas and suggestions to ensure your ongoing success, fulfillment, and empowerment. We'll also outline our most basic self-care tool, the *Care Cycle*. This simple step-by-step method is one practical way you can stay engaged in the process of learning how to keep yourself well cared for.

Remember that *you* are the one responsible for making sure you feel good about living in your skin. If that isn't working, don't look to anyone else to make it different or better for you. God is counting on *you* to care for you.

Success in Self-Care

When done well, caring for yourself is not selfish at all but is, in fact, the most responsible thing you can do for your relationship with your spouse. Getting over the objection that self-care is selfish is the first step.

Many of the brothers and sisters in Christ we've discussed this with continue to ask, "Okay, I understand the significance of good self-care, but what does it look like practically?" That's a reasonable question to ask in a culture that doesn't teach the principle of balancing self-care with investing responsibly in others. Let's start by applying that core truth in practical ways.

Make It Personal

The details of self-care will always look a little different for each one of us. We are each uniquely created, and while we can get self-care ideas from others, in the end, what works for me (Bob) will not always work for you. Many of the things that keep me healthy and operating at peak performance are not necessarily best for Jenni. The same is true of Tara and Vince. Each of us must strive to understand what helps us thrive individually so we can bring our best selves to the world and those we love. The goal for each of us is to feel confident that we are living true to who we were created to be. From there we can most effectively support and encourage others to do the same.

One example of this became crystal clear to me (Tara) early in my marriage to Vince. For him to relax, it's important that all cleaning and maintenance tasks are completed—and he doesn't mind working hard to achieve that state. I, on the other hand, feel overwhelmed with to-do lists that never seem to end. Early in our marriage, I tried to either get Vince to take breaks and relax or push myself to do more to keep up with him. I wanted to be a good partner, but it never felt like we completed the work. I was wearing myself down and becoming resentful until I realized that I could give myself permission to be who I'm wired to be. I can still be highly productive much of the time, but I also know I need regular downtime so I can get all the things on my list done. I no longer pressure Vince to rest with me, and he doesn't push me to keep going at his pace.

Make Space

Responsible self-care always builds in some margin. If there's no time and space for self-care, it won't happen. Fighting hard—often very hard—to create a little breathing room will improve your personal health while simultaneously modeling responsible living for others.

It's difficult, we know. We talk with many individuals whose lives are so packed with activities and responsibilities that they see no way to make any meaningful time for themselves. In fact, they are running so close to the edge, it's as if they're living paycheck to paycheck. Everything works if nothing unexpected pops up. If someone's finances are that tight, one surprise can instantly overdraw their bank account. Too many surprises in close proximity could mean bankruptcy. The same sort of thing can happen to us emotionally, spiritually, physically, and mentally (ESPM). Our resources can easily get overdrawn, and we can become personally bankrupt.

In a world as unpredictable as ours, *not* living consistently on the edge leaves room for the "expected unexpected" to happen and gives us the space to respond in wise and healthy ways.

Make It Balanced

Everyone needs to have some sense of balance in their lives. But that's often a difficult goal. There are so many aspects of our personal lives that need to be balanced—work life and home life, work and play, exertion and rest, social time and alone time. And as couples, we need to balance spending time together and spending time apart, working together and working on our own, and so on.

In keeping with our God-designed differences—our personalities, preferences, and temperaments—what constitutes balance will also vary from person to person. Balance does not necessarily mean a fifty-fifty split in every area of our lives and relationships. For example, many introverts would feel terrible if they tried to maintain an even split between social interaction and private time. An introvert might need 75 percent private time and 25 percent social interaction to experience a life that feels balanced and healthy. An extrovert might prefer the opposite.

Our friends Dr. Greg Smalley and his wife, Erin, offer a simple framework for balance in their book *Reconnected*.[1] As we look for ways to balance the many aspects of life and marriage, the Smalleys encourage us to focus on two simple questions: What brings you *life*? And what brings you *rest*? In other words, what are the activities that make you feel fully alive, inspired, and energized? And what most effectively allows you to rest, recharge, and get refreshed? This simple model is kind of like breathing. Breathing in and out is a foundation for sustaining life. In, then out. Repeat. One without the other won't work. Ideally, the same applies in our model of a balanced life.

How do you best encourage patterns that give you a sense of being vital and alive, so that life routinely feels as if you've just had a wonderful cup of coffee? The energy is flowing, and you're ready to go. Our Lord created your life and wants you to experience it fully—"Thus says the Lord God to these bones: Behold, I will cause breath to enter you, and you shall live" (Ezekiel 37:5). Life-giving activities *invigorate* you, bringing passion, hope, creativity, and joy to your day. These are experiences that make your heart come alive!

We could list thousands of examples here, though only some would stir your heart. The key is finding out what fills *you* up. Is it hiking in the mountains, walking along the beach, swimming, surfing, or snorkeling? Maybe it's spending time on your favorite hobbies—fishing, golf, photography, cooking, or some other area of interest. Or trying something new, such as taking a class, conquering a fear, or serving on a mission trip. Perhaps you enjoy mentoring underprivileged youth, serving with a charitable organization, joining the board of a nonprofit, or starting your own business or outreach ministry. Although these activities can leave you feeling exhausted, they can also leave you feeling satisfied and alive. The goal is not rest but to come back *full*!

Remember that the key is *balance*. Some people can get so pumped up doing activities they love that, in a way, they become adrenaline junkies and lose their personal and relational balance. Frequently this occurs at the expense of important relationships or personal well-being. Be on the lookout for evidence you've slipped out of balance, even as you remember that feeling alive and full is a nonnegotiable.

So with balance in clear focus, let's shift to the other side of the living-well coin. We need plenty of energy to engage in the things that bring life, but we also need to recharge after we're done. Finding ways to rest, refresh, and rejuvenate is vital for living well—and it's close to the heart of God. Jesus said,

> "Come to me, all who labor and are heavy laden, and
> I will give you rest. Take my yoke upon you, and learn
> from me, for I am gentle and lowly in heart, and you
> will find rest for your souls. For my yoke is easy, and
> my burden is light."
> MATTHEW 11:28-30

Unfortunately, too many people live hectic, stress-filled lives. They often feel as if they're carrying the weight of the world on their shoulders. *There's no time for rest.* But rest is essential for overall health and well-being. This also needs to be nonnegotiable.

Rest is ceasing work or movement to relax and refresh ourselves, or to recover strength. It allows our bodies to recuperate from the demands we put on them. There are many ways to rest and recharge. Obviously, the basics must include getting adequate sleep—seven and a half to nine hours a night is the usual recommendation from doctors—as well as eating nutritious food, the basic fuel for our systems. But after those basics, the list gets more personal.

For some of us (even men), the ultimate way to rest and recharge might include a day at the spa, a manicure, or a pedicure. Others might be more interested in reading a book, playing video games, lounging around in pajamas, going fishing or hunting, watching a favorite TV show, listening to music, gardening, enjoying arts and crafts, praying, meditating on God's Word, or completing a puzzle.

Regardless of the activity (or *lack* of activity), we each need to pay attention to what helps us recharge our batteries.

Sometimes, adding a nap to a busy schedule can feel like the epitome of luxury. Perhaps you're a world-class power napper. A ten- to twenty-minute nap can create an immediate energy boost. Some cultures value longer naps and even build afternoon rest time into everyone's workday. Those of us who appreciate the gift of a good nap are often baffled when young children see it as a form of punishment!

For some of us, rest is best achieved by entering a playful space. That might mean an activity, such as playing a game or some type of sport. Those endeavors are certainly types of play, but as we have learned, the playfulness that helps a person rest is based more on attitude than on a specific activity. You can bring a playful spirit into almost anything, turning even mundane pursuits into leisurely and restful activities.

Again, find the playful activity that works best for you—one that lifts your spirits instead of draining you. Few things do more to lift our spirits than laughter. A good laugh can help your whole body release tension and relax.

Attend to Your Whole Self

A big key for living a balanced life is making sure every part of yourself is adequately attended to. You are more than just a physical being. You have a mind, a spirit, and a heart as well. To live your best life, every part needs attention and care.

Your body is the most obvious place to start because it screams the loudest when neglected. The health concerns of carrying excess weight are well known, but we also know that being underweight and undernourished can create problems. In addition to rest and nutrition, our bodies need regular exercise to operate at peak performance. Even something as simple as breaking up your day with short walks as opposed to sitting or standing in one position for too long can make a significant difference in your physical health. There are also apps that alert us when we've been still too long and it's time to get up and move.

Scripture instructs us to take care of ourselves because our bodies are temples of the Holy Spirit (1 Corinthians 3:16; 6:19; Ephesians 2:22). God wants us to care for His temple. When children don't take good care of themselves, it saddens parents. It also saddens God to see His children not taking care of themselves and suffering the consequences.

Beyond our bodies, though, many people don't think too deeply about what good self-care looks like. (Remember ESPM?) Our minds also need attention to function optimally. Not caring for our minds by keeping them active can contribute to mental decline and disorders like Alzheimer's disease and dementia. Exercising your brain means staying engaged in learning, exploring, sharing ideas with others, reading, writing, and a host of other activities. There are even brain-training video games and smartphone apps you can use. Brain exercise is not unlike physical exercise. Exercising your body requires intentional *physical* activity. Exercising your mind requires intentional *mental* activity.

Caring for your spiritual well-being is also essential for overall health. We're all spiritual beings—whether or not we recognize this reality. God (a spiritual being) created you to be like Him (with a spirit) and to live in a continual relationship with Him (a spiritual activity). Acknowledging this fundamental truth about yourself is the first step toward becoming spiritually healthy. In chapter 4, we highlighted several spiritual disciplines to help you develop and maintain your connection with God. These practices are also effective for strengthening your spiritual health.

Last, but certainly not least, is the importance of attending to our emotional health—our hearts. We wanted to cover this last because it is normally the least understood, and perhaps the least well-attended, aspect of our being. Yes, God implores us, "Above all else, guard your heart, for everything you do flows from it" (Proverbs 4:23, NIV). But beyond simple protection, to live a balanced life means attending to the needs of your heart with respect and care. This requires understanding the importance and function of your feelings. When you fully appreciate the role your heart is meant to play in life, love, and service to God, you can more easily find the motivation to give it the attention it deserves.

God created our emotions to function as critical data for effective personal care and the substance of intimate connection in love and life, which we'll discuss later in this book. The significance of emotional self-care to overall health and well-being has been gaining prominence in our world over the last number of decades. In fact, since the 1990s, the importance of *emotional intelligence* (EQ) has received increasing attention. This is distinct from a person's IQ, the generally fixed mental capacity (intelligence) an individual is born with. By contrast, EQ is a type of intelligence that can be developed over time.

In his book *Emotional Intelligence*, Daniel Goleman, an American psychologist, outlined the core components of this capacity: self-control, persistence, and the ability to motivate ourselves, combined with the ability to empathize and read emotions in others; and, crucially, an ability to understand our core emotional processes.[2]

In the next section, we'll focus on the Care Cycle and dig into how developing our EQ can help bring our lives into better balance. But caring well for yourself emotionally by increasing your EQ initially requires taking time to tune into your heart and identify *what* you are feeling. Ideally, it means being able to name your emotions. From there you can begin to understand what your feelings reveal about your wants and needs so you can assume the full responsibility of caring for yourself more effectively.

The Care Cycle

The Care Cycle is a simple five-step tool that will help you understand yourself better emotionally and then develop effective strategies to care for yourself in ways that promote your well-being and recharge your batteries. Not surprisingly, the potential relationship-building aspect of emotional intelligence includes learning healthy ways to express yourself emotionally and share your feelings with select others. A meaningful, intimate connection with another person will always be an open-heart-to-open-heart engagement, and feelings are the substance of that connection.

We assume that everyone reading this book has had some success in caring well for themselves. Yet many aren't able to pinpoint what they do that really works for them. The Care Cycle outlines an easy step-by-step process most people can follow for successful self-care.

As we discussed in the previous chapter, effective self-care is both proactive and reactive. The five steps of the Care Cycle work both ways—when you're attending to regular proactive maintenance, and when you're caught in the Reactive Cycle.

Used proactively, the Care Cycle can help you more clearly understand your wants and needs so you are better equipped to live a healthy and empowered life. With consistent use, you will typically feel seen, validated, understood, and cared for. When you are regularly "cared up," as we like to call it, you will likely find that your buttons are less sensitive, and it's far easier to get out of a reactive cycle when it happens.

Since this tool is a cycle, it's intended for you to repeat as many times as needed. It really is a feedback loop, which means that as you work through each step, you'll note what works and what doesn't. Then you'll feed that information back into the cycle and adjust what you're doing so you can improve your self-care. Keep repeating the cycle until the outcome is one you like and you feel cared up.

At the start, we encourage people to work through each step in order. If you realize at any point that you didn't complete an earlier step, pause what you're doing and go back to that step. Once you've finished, you can return to where you were in the cycle. As you become more familiar with the Care Cycle, you'll likely find that some steps become easier, while others take more time and effort. We hope this cycle will become second nature to you, and you'll feel well cared for in all ESPM aspects of your everyday experience. How nice would that be?

Following is a basic diagram of the Care Cycle that includes the five steps, or five As, we'll explore in detail:

Care Cycle

Step 1: Aware

To effectively care for yourself, you first must recognize that something is going on *inside* you. Physically, this could be as simple as your stomach growling, telling you that you're hungry. This internal alarm bell or signal is part of the system God designed to alert the responsible caregiver (you) that something needs attention. For most people, the practice of recognizing that alarm bell is foreign. Many believe we should just ignore pesky, unreliable emotions. But God created emotions to provide the data we need to effectively care for ourselves as He intended. So the first part of expert self-care is to become more aware of your emotions and the physical signs that often accompany them. If you're normally tuned out when it comes to your inner world, you need to start tuning in.

In the last chapter, when we discussed how to break the Reactive Cycle, we noted that the first essential step is to wake up and recognize that you have been triggered. That is the Aware step of the Care Cycle. When you start using this cycle, you may need to work on noticing your external reactions, which are usually reliable indicators that you are being triggered. But with practice, you can shift your attention to your internal signals. Clinical therapist Deb Dana notes that roughly 80 percent of the information about what is happening in our bodies is transmitted from the body to the brain (a "bottom-up" flow of information), whereas only 20 percent is transmitted from the brain to our bodies.[3] So the benefit of tuning in to your body's signals is that you can get the needed information more quickly.

EXERCISE

Think about a reactive moment and ask yourself, *What happens in my body that lets me know I'm triggered?* It's a little different for everyone, and some people may not feel anything, but try to be aware of what is happening inside you. Notice where distressing emotions show up in your body. Do you recognize any physiological sensations? For example, your heart may be racing, or your breathing may increase and become shallow. Are you perspiring, or does your skin feel clammy? Has your mouth gone dry? Are you feeling hot or cold? Do your muscles feel tight or constricted? Perhaps you feel numb or dead inside. Is your stomach churning or sinking, or does it feel as if butterflies are flying around in there? Do you notice any other sensations? (For a list of sensation words, turn to appendix C, "Body Sensations.")

Paying attention to your internal signaling system is a key aspect of learning to regulate your emotions and calm yourself. We all developed patterns and procedural maps for our emotional responses before our brains fully matured. So you may need to remind yourself that you are an adult now, and you have more resources to keep yourself safe than you did back when these patterns and maps were created. Paying attention to what's going on in your body is the first step in rewriting those outdated maps. The idea is to notice physical and emotional states without judging them as bad or good. Simply observe what is going on as neutral information.

The dashboards in our cars have several lights and indicators. When the gas light comes on, it doesn't mean your car is in trouble; it simply means that you need to fill the tank. But if you ignore that signal because it's inconvenient and you expect it to just go away on its own, you'll soon have a bigger issue to deal with. Similarly, when the check-engine light comes on, it's not always clear what might be going on with the car, but the signal informs you to explore further to ensure your car can be restored to proper functioning. Body sensations and emotional responses function like your internal dashboards.

While most people can learn to feel comfortable with this first step of awareness and can easily begin the next step, sometimes we can become too wound up or dysregulated to move on. If you're aware of that important emotional response, great! We've included the STOP Method in appendix D to help ground you so you can transition into the second step of the Care Cycle when you're ready.

Step 2: Accept

There are two components of the Accept step. First is accepting the *responsibility* for self-care. At Focus on the Family, we often say, "My heart, my job." But since we are more than just emotional beings, we prefer to say, "Caring for my whole self (ESPM) is my job!" Fully accepting this responsibility indicates that you're showing up like a fully functioning adult.

Julie from Tara's research reflected, "My big takeaway was [that] I was so tired and angry, but I never stopped to take care of myself. I expected David to do that." Can you relate? Once Julie accepted the job of caring for herself, she felt empowered and cared for. When she took the pressure off David (who was never supposed to have that responsibility), their relationship felt safer for both of them. So one important part of the Accept step is taking your power back by taking on the responsibility to care for yourself.

The second component of this step is often where the cycle breaks down for most people, particularly when they're triggered: We also need to accept our *feelings*. Generally, each of us is aware when our buttons are being pushed and we're experiencing emotions. Often, we don't like having those feelings. What do we *want* to do with unpleasant emotions? Make them go away, of course! That is obviously *not* accepting our feelings.

Yes, it's natural that we'd want to push away unpleasant or scary emotions, but acceptance is about welcoming them for a short visit, having an open and curious attitude toward them, and not judging what they might be trying to tell us. Why? Again, God designed our emotions to contain all the data we need to understand self-care. It's essential we pay attention to that information.

Can you imagine choosing to ignore the warning signals on your car's dashboard because you don't like them? It would significantly impact your ability to make informed decisions about the maintenance of your vehicle and could end up costing you a whole lot more in the long run. When you ignore your emotions or try to get rid of these vital nonverbal signals, you lose two-thirds of your God-given power to live your best life. Acceptance is about taking back your power, embracing your responsibility for self-care, and paying close attention to all the amazing information God has designed your body to give you to succeed.

Step 3: Allow

You weren't created to live in isolation. You were created for relationship with others and with God. So attempting to care well for yourself without God and other people in your life is to set yourself at odds with God's design. The Allow step is about asking God to be with you and assist you in the self-care journey. He wants you to be responsible, but He doesn't want or expect you to do it alone.

So when you've been triggered in a heated moment with your spouse, you might pray something like this:

*Lord, please help me calm down, think clearly, and
remember that my spouse is not the enemy but the helpmate
You gave me. Help me recognize Satan's lies and schemes and
how he wants me to see my spouse as the enemy. Help me lay
down my anger, hurt, and frustration and be open to the
presence of Your Spirit. Allow me to experience Your peace,
patience, kindness, and gentleness. Help me remember I'm
loved and forgiven, and fill me with Your love and mercy so
I can extend it to myself and my spouse. Help me have eyes to
see and ears to hear and understand my own heart, to notice
what I'm feeling and where it might be coming from, and to
have understanding for my spouse's heart as well. Give me the
humility to acknowledge how I might be contributing to our
challenges. Help me remember that my spouse and I are on
the same team.*

The power of Allow is in seeking and receiving God's help and
empowerment. In taking this step, you are surrendering your will
to His and allowing Him to guide you.

There's another part to this step. Since God created you to
live in a loving family and community, the Allow step includes
asking and allowing other people to come alongside and care for
you. It's often helpful to share your internal exploration with
another person who engages with you in a way that makes you
feel heard. They may have great ideas or a different perspective
to share with you. As with any counsel you receive, thought-
fully ponder it, paying attention to your thoughts and emotions.
Bring it to the Lord and ask for His wisdom in response to what
others share.

A human helper can certainly be your spouse. But if you want
outside assistance, be careful to choose someone who is always for

you, your spouse, *and* your marriage. That person should be able to remain curious and nonjudgmental, without trying to jump in and fix things. This could be a safe friend, a pastor, or a trained therapist. If you do reach out to someone else for help, remember that it is never *their* responsibility to make things better for you. It is still your job in your own yard. All outside human helpers are 100 percent volunteer, including your spouse.

Step 4: Attend

Next is the primary work step in the Care Cycle. The first three steps can proceed quickly and may feel something like this:

- *Wow, I'm triggered! Taking care of me is my job, and I'm on it.*
- *These feelings are full of the information I need, and I'm listening.*
- *God, I need Your help right now to figure out what's going on and what caring for myself looks like in this situation.*

The Attend step is where you figure out what is going on and what you need to be well cared for. It's a proactive space where you attend to yourself and identify what you need to remain full, whole, and healthy emotionally, spiritually, physically, and mentally (ESPM). You'll begin by seeking to understand and comfort the fears, wounds, desires, and needs in your life. You may hang out here for a while!

It's important to start with an open, curious attitude toward yourself. Acknowledge your emotional needs in a nonjudgmental way. Allow yourself to feel them, simply observing and remaining curious about them. You are preparing to mine the information, extracting what you need to care for yourself.

From that accepting attitude, you'll move to the exploration stage and begin asking yourself questions as you search for what you need to be well cared up. The questions that follow are some of the most commonly asked ones that usually yield the most fruit. You may think of others that resonate more or are especially relevant to what you're exploring.

What am I feeling? In the first step, you may have become aware of some emotions, but now it's time to go deeper and put a name and face to them. Initially, it might be easier to simply identify one of seven general emotions that may be coming up: joy, fear, sadness, anger, shame, guilt, or loneliness. But ultimately, there is great value in finding words that capture both the feeling and the intensity. For instance, are you feeling sad—or are you disappointed, heartbroken, or devastated? These feelings are related, but they clearly describe different levels of emotion, and you will likely attend to each one a bit differently. We have included a list of feeling words in appendix E to refer to if needed, or you can look at the feelings list you compiled for the Reactive Cycle.

As you focus on what's going on emotionally, begin "trying on" the feeling words to see which ones fit best, like trying on clothes you're thinking about purchasing. When you find a word that fits, you'll instantly think, *Yes! That's what I'm feeling.*

Is this a familiar emotion? Have you felt this way before, perhaps at other times in this relationship? What about in other relationships or situations? Does it remind you of any past hurts in your life—maybe in childhood or during your young-adult years? How old do you feel when you let yourself connect with this emotion? The answers to these questions will often reveal why the emotion or reaction is as intense as it is.

Our brains always make sense of new situations by looking for associations with existing neural pathways. When an association is found, our brains quickly lump the new situation together with existing pathways so we can move on to the next thing. So if you've felt an emotion before, even though the situation may be new, it's likely that your brain has recalled other times throughout your life when you felt this way. If previous situations were negative or unpleasant, your brain won't necessarily remind you of the original event, but you may react as if all these situations are related.

For example, if Jenni says something that taps an unconscious emotional memory of something my (Bob's) mother said that bothered me, it can transport me back to that moment, or similar moments. Suddenly I'm feeling the impact of what Jenni said, combined with the pain of what my mom said back then. I'm rarely conscious of it at first, but the feelings are more intense because I'm experiencing the combined impact of both situations, *not* just what Jenni said. All I'm aware of in that moment is what Jenni said and that it was upsetting. Pausing to ask if this is a familiar feeling can enable me to see the connection. With this new information, I might say to Jenni, "That comment hurt a lot, partly because of what you said but also because it reminded me of . . ."

Recognizing connections with the past is not intended to dismiss your emotional response to the present situation, but it does allow you to better understand why it triggered you so intensely. The process also gives you more information you can use to better care for yourself. No matter what comes up, your heart needs your compassion and validation—*Oh, now it makes sense why I had those feelings and reacted that way.* It gives you a feeling of being seen, understood, and validated.

Am I causing or increasing this feeling? Most of us are pretty good at stirring up our emotions, keeping them spinning, or shutting them down in such a way that we end up feeling worse. Even though Sadie, from Tara's research, felt hopeful at the end of her intensive work with her husband, when she got home, she returned to her negative thinking patterns and found herself spiraling into depression. She kept rehearsing the many ways Bill had hurt her and how he couldn't be trusted. Even though he was working on changing, the situation didn't change for Sadie until she decided it was time to stop spinning in her pain and, instead, start caring for her emotions and making efforts to connect with Bill. Only then did their marriage begin to heal.

This question is about focusing on a real, possibly painful honesty with yourself. *Hey, God, I may need Your help with this one.* If you've gotten used to beating yourself up, rehearsing hurts, or dumping "You should have . . ." and "Why didn't you . . . ?" on yourself, you're likely making things worse. Even so, don't judge yourself for that. These strategies were all you had when you were younger. Some of these tactics may even have helped you survive what would have been unbearable otherwise. But now you're different. You are not a helpless child anymore. As an adult, you are physically bigger, and your brain has fully developed. You're also independent and have more options now.

The more you reveal here, the more helpful information this question will yield! If it turns out that you're causing your painful feelings, you now possess the power to single-handedly stop making yourself feel worse. Now, that *is* empowering!

What is true? Frequently, with a little focused reflection, you can discover that the beliefs and conclusions driving your emotions are not true. Yet you're operating as if they were! While feelings by themselves are usually not right or wrong, or good or bad, *beliefs* can absolutely be true or false. And they can generate powerful feelings.

For example, if you grew up constantly hearing comments

like "What's wrong with you?" or "You're useless!" or "You'll never amount to anything," firm beliefs about your core worth and value might have lodged in your young psyche, fueling your emotional sensitivities. As we learned in the Reactive Cycle, these internal beliefs are buttons or triggers. When something or someone pushes your buttons, you may experience intense emotions springing from a belief about yourself.

One of our friends shared this story:

> I grew up with a family that always used positive affirmations and strong discipline. The more I excelled, the more positive the atmosphere was for me. But it made things very difficult for my little sister, who was five years younger than me. Everybody, including family and teachers, expected her to excel like me, and even though she could have easily surpassed me in all areas, she decided to rebel. She developed negative beliefs about herself that greatly impacted her. The resulting emotions carried over into her adult life and eventually caused her marriage, friendships, and relationship with God to fail.

Once you've identified the beliefs lurking in your subconscious mind, you need to ask yourself, *Is that belief actually true?* In our friend's example, the questions might be something like this: *Am I really useless in Christ? Is it true I'll never amount to anything?*

Ask God to convict you of any thoughts, beliefs, or behaviors you may not be seeing. Might any filters you're looking through be distorting your perspective? Are you looking at any shadow monsters? Remember, the Holy Spirit convicts us for our benefit. He's there to help us grow, not to shame us. You can't change or correct what you are unaware of, and false beliefs can feel painfully true when they go unexamined. The enemy loves to feed our minds with lies that stir our emotions. And feelings, by themselves, don't actually know what is true and what is false. Our rational brains determine that for us.

Next, move to broader, more general truths: *What is true about me as a person?* Consider the Be List qualities you identified in chapter 3 and ask yourself, *What is true about me from God's perspective? What is true about God's love for me?* (Check out the Scriptures in appendix F for good reminders of how God really sees you.)

Also consider exploring truths about your spouse. You can just as easily develop false beliefs about others, and they can generate powerful feelings too. Ask yourself these questions: *What do I know to be true about my spouse when I'm not feeling hurt or angry because of something they said or did? What is true about my spouse from God's perspective? What is true about our marriage overall? Am I starting to see what has been happening from a new perspective? And am I starting to see new possibilities because I'm caring for my wounds?*

What do I want and who do I want to be? Hopefully you're starting to settle on some answers as you work through this Attend step. Ask yourself, *What do I really want in this situation? What attributes do I want to "put on" right now so I can be the person God created me to be?*

The answers to these questions will provide the knowledge you'll need as you transition to the final step, which is acting on the goals you've identified. Creating an action plan to develop attributes and action steps will help you achieve your goals. This plan will allow you to respond to conflict from your grounded adult brain rather than reacting like a wounded child or a protective teen.

Step 5: Act

The basic principle of this step is simple: Just do it! Equipped with all the information about who you really are, as well as what you want and need to feel well cared for, you'll start taking real steps to care for yourself based on the information you gathered and the action plan you developed during the fourth step.

You've probably noticed some positive developments while working through the earlier steps of the Care Cycle. But it's important to remember that significant change doesn't come unless you follow through with *doing* something different and better, deciding on an action step and then trying it out.

After trying the action step, you can cycle back to the first step of the Care Cycle and notice how your body is responding. Has anything changed? Are you feeling cared for, or is there room for improvement? Are there other areas that need care?

If you feel anything less than awesome, consider working through the five As again. Cycle through the steps as many times as you need to ensure that you've done everything possible to feel cared up. As you get used to caring for yourself, you may be able to move through the process more quickly. In fact, you may not need to start from the absolute beginning every time. What works for you in one situation may apply to the next situation, so you'll build on previous success. Some circumstances are just easier and don't require a lot of deep introspection. The main goal is to make sure you always feel well cared for, that everyone around you will benefit from the work you've done, and that God will be delighted to see His child cared for and equipped for life.

As we wrap up our discussion, take a few minutes to review this more detailed illustration of the Care Cycle:

Care Cycle

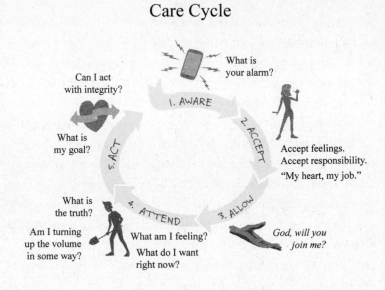

7

FORGIVENESS
AND FREEDOM

IT'S TIME TO ADDRESS ONE LAST AREA that often binds us and depletes our personal power: forgiveness—or rather, the lack of it.

It's difficult to let go of resentment and bitterness. When you're not able to forgive someone, you inadvertently shut off parts of yourself from receiving God's love and provision. You're not acting as the love-filled vessel God created you to be. Unforgiveness effectively shuts the door to your heart. While you may have intended to close your heart only toward another person, slamming the door also shuts God out—or at least closes off areas within you where you truly need His love to flow. Thus, you're unable to receive the full power available to you from your source, and you're inhibited from being your best self. What's worse, a heart closed off to love essentially poisons you from the inside.

Is forgiveness primarily a Christian value? Certainly it's a foundational principle of the faith, but the need to give and receive forgiveness seems to be wired into humanity. Research has revealed the detrimental effects of unforgiveness, regardless of whether a person knows God. According to the Mayo Clinic, unforgiveness may contribute in big ways to depression, irritability, and anxiety, as well as spreading anger and bitterness to other relationships.[1]

As important as forgiveness is to our overall health and well-being, there really isn't a universally agreed-upon understanding of forgiveness. What is it, exactly? Scripture has a lot to say about forgiveness, and the potential impact of unforgiveness on life and marriage is so significant that sharing some basic thoughts and strategies on the subject is essential. We hope this will bring you some new perspective and greater freedom from bonds that can bog down your marriage.

Before we dig into this topic, it's important to clarify one area of frequent confusion: the relationship of trust and reconciliation to forgiveness. Trust and reconciliation are obviously related to forgiveness (and to each other), but they aren't necessarily *prerequisites* for forgiveness. What does that mean? Many people assume that true forgiveness necessitates that we first restore trust and reconciliation in a broken relationship. However, there are real situations in life where trust and (the appearance of) reconciliation are unwise and sometimes dangerous. However, it is possible to forgive someone without trusting them. You can also forgive even if your relationship isn't fully repaired. So choosing between forgiving and living in sin and forgiving and living in harm's way is a false choice.

What Is Forgiveness?

First, let's define what we mean by *forgiveness* to make sure we're all on the same page. Forgiveness is, fundamentally, about canceling a debt. In a relational context, something has been done, or not done, that has hurt or violated one or more persons in some way. The result is a *relational debt* that requires some kind of payment to make things right. Rather than managing this debt ourselves, we (the injured parties) release it to God, trusting in His justice. For believers saved by God's grace alone, it's prudent to look to Him rather than attempting to righteously manage these debts on our own. God will either punish the offender or pay the debt Himself, but that is ultimately up to Him. When you forgive someone, you release your efforts to be in control. You free yourself from holding on to something you cannot righteously rectify by exacting payment.

The apostle Paul reminds us, "Do not take revenge, my dear friends, but leave room for God's wrath, for it is written: 'It is mine to avenge; I will repay,' says the Lord" (Romans 12:19, NIV). We often self-righteously believe that others deserve punishment, and that might be true. But God is the only One who can truly bring justice, for His understanding of all our sins is complete. In the face of injustice, it's easy to forget that we, too, have sinned and deserve to be punished. If justice were really served, every one of us would hang on the cross that Jesus bore for our sins.

When you allow yourself to remember God's amazing mercy toward you and how much you've been forgiven, it's easier to forgive others.

Forgiveness Isn't Easy

Easier does not mean *easy*. One misconception many Christians hold is that because God has forgiven us, it *should* be easy for us to forgive others. But consider what was required of God to cancel our debts. We sinned and incurred a debt that needed to be paid because it created a divide between us and God. That divide was so great, we couldn't remedy it ourselves. But because of His unfathomable love for us, He devised a brilliant but costly way to reconcile our debt and restore our relationship with Him. He sent Jesus to endure the full punishment we deserved so there would no longer be anything standing between us and our Lord—"For God so loved the world, that he gave his only Son, that whoever believes in him should not perish but have eternal life" (John 3:16).

God the Father allowed Jesus to be brutally crucified to pay the entire debt for all humanity. And remember, Jesus agreed to this plan—it wasn't some horrible, cosmic child abuse. Our human minds and hearts can't imagine what that was like for Jesus, the Father, or the Holy Spirit, who otherwise have always lived in perpetual unity and open connection. We might be able to understand Jesus' prayer in the garden of Gethsemane, where he asked God the Father, "If you are willing, remove this cup from me," before obediently yielding to the Father's plan (Luke 22:42).

God knows that forgiveness likely won't come easily for any of us. He wants us to look to Him, depend on Him, and work with Him, following in His footsteps. Surrendering ourselves into God's arms enables us to receive undeserved release and reconciliation as we draw near to Him and let Him administer justice and judgment as He sees fit.

As healing as forgiveness can be for the offender, the freedom and power for the offended are off the charts! Forgiveness is first about releasing *yourself* from the burden of holding on to offenses. Some people think unforgiveness can protect them from being hurt the same way again, but it just doesn't work that way. Unforgiveness imprisons us in victimhood, as we view present events through the filter of past injustices.

That is not to say you haven't been victimized. We've all been hurt, and some have had it worse than most. But being a victim in the past is very different from constantly feeling like a victim and living like one in the present. In a very real sense, unforgiveness is when *you* repeat the offense *within yourself* over and over, believing that keeping the wound fresh and bleeding will help you somehow. Instead, it slowly and effectively depletes you of joy, hope, and any kind of resiliency.

We have worked with many survivors of tragedies and traumas, and we've witnessed how differently people deal with those experiences emotionally and psychologically. Some have been so traumatized, they've become largely nonfunctional. They can't manage their lives or relationships, and certainly not their emotions. Others find ways to overcome the most horrific events and still find health and healing. A major variable is the degree to which this second group is able and willing to forgive, let go, and move toward healing and personal power.

God doesn't want your offender to have the power to continue harming you. You are His child, and He wants you whole, healthy, and fully empowered, regardless of how embattled or oppressed you've been. Again, please hear that we aren't saying the offense and resulting pain are insignificant. They matter deeply! But God doesn't want you to stay stuck there. He doesn't want you defeated. He wants you to be victorious and empowered. He wants you to win with Him!

After allowing God to be the justice keeper and help you find a way to let go of the offense—often slowly, with prayer, wrestling, openness, and curiosity—you can begin to see your offender's perspective. This perspective shift in no way makes the offense acceptable. But it does allow you to see another person's humanity and brokenness. It can also help you forgive more completely, taking your healing to another level.

Dr. Everett Worthington, a Christian who pioneered forgiveness research, experienced the power of refocusing his perspective after suffering an unimaginable crime. His mother was molested and brutally murdered when she startled two teenagers breaking into her home on New Year's Eve. Then his brother, who discovered the crime scene, committed suicide a few years later, unable to manage the horror of what he had seen.

As Dr. Worthington wrestled through the process of forgiveness in the aftermath of his mother's murder and his brother's death, he wrote, "The essence of the forgiveness model is taking the hard step of trying to see things through the offender's eyes. Through prayer, I could see the young man's fear of prison and anger at having his plans spoiled. Being able to empathize with him didn't mean I accepted what he had done. But it did help me forgive him."[2] Worthington made the difficult but powerful discovery that seeing the humanity in others softens our hearts and empowers us to forgive. He clearly had just cause to never forgive the person responsible for both of his loved ones' deaths. But he was also wise enough to know that he would not do himself, the Lord, or the Kingdom of God any favors by remaining locked in the prison of unforgiveness. (For more information and resources from Worthington's research, visit evworthington-forgiveness.com.)

Time Alone Doesn't Heal

Another misconception about forgiveness is that time will heal our hearts and bring about forgiveness naturally. So if we've been mistreated or offended, we just need to allow forgiveness to magically happen over time. That is rarely the case. Forgiveness is an *intentional* sacrifice we must consciously make. Someone owes us, and we let it go. We cancel the emotional debt and walk away.

If you don't intentionally let something go, time will often intensify and warp hurt feelings until they fester and poison you.

This poison becomes a barrier between you and God that can hinder your ability to tap into His love and power. It is the curse that keeps on giving. You were hurt originally, and then by hanging on to the offense, you just keep losing and losing and losing more.

When Jesus was teaching His disciples about prayer, He instructed them to pray for God's forgiveness, just as they forgave others. He then went on to say, "For if you forgive other people when they sin against you, your heavenly Father will also forgive you. But if you do not forgive others their sins, your Father will not forgive your sins" (Matthew 6:14-15, NIV). Forgiving others is directly connected to receiving God's forgiveness, and we desperately need God's ongoing grace to keep that life-giving relational channel with Him open and clear.

We often ask people, "When is the moment God forgives you?" The typical response is "When we ask Him to forgive us." But God's ultimate forgiveness happened at the cross, and the moment you accept His gift of forgiveness, you are fully set free. The debt has already been paid in full.

However, if you refuse to offer forgiveness to others as He has done with you, in essence, it's as if *you* have erected a wall between yourself and God, and it's now *your* responsibility to take it down. As we said earlier, unforgiveness closes the door to your heart, and you are the keeper of that door. Forgiving others as you have been forgiven is one way you can keep your door wide open to God.

God doesn't withhold Himself from us. Remember the description of God's love in 1 Corinthians 13 that we shared earlier? Since God *is* love, He is patient and kind, and He never gives up on us. He will always enter an open heart willing to receive Him. Yet each of us has the power to shut Him out and keep the door closed.

He will respect that choice, whether or not it's in our best interest. Choose to keep your heart open to God's love and forgiveness.

Forgiveness doesn't mean excusing the wrongs others have done to you. As we noted earlier, the offense and resulting pain aren't insignificant. They're very real and need to be validated and cared for so your healing and growth can continue. And forgiveness alone is often not enough to bring them about. This is where a skillful application of the Care Cycle is especially valuable. Later in this chapter, we'll share some additional steps to forgiveness, and beyond, that can truly help past wounds heal.

Forgiveness Is Not Forgetting

The idea of forgiving and forgetting isn't really possible unless we have very poor memories. When intense emotions and experiences get wired into our memories, as is usually the case when we're faced with something hurtful, we do need to forgive. But we won't automatically forget the pain. It doesn't come naturally to us.

Does God forget when He forgives? Psalm 103:12 says, "As far as the east is from the west, so far does he remove our transgressions from us." We also read in Jeremiah 31:34, "No longer shall each one teach his neighbor and each his brother, saying, 'Know the LORD,' for they shall all know me, from the least of them to the greatest, declares the LORD. For I will forgive their iniquity, and I will remember their sin no more." God doesn't necessarily seem to forget sins the way we think of forgetting, but we know that He removes sin from us and doesn't look at us in light of our wrongdoing.

Interestingly, the psalmist didn't say, "As far as the north is from the south . . . ," because that is a limited distance. If you begin heading east from your home and continue going east, you will never hit a point where you begin heading west instead. So God will never look upon you through the lens of your sin. He remembers but chooses to look at you through the lens of Jesus' sacrifice instead. First Corinthians 13 tells us that God (who is love) "keeps no record of wrongs" (verse 5, NIV). Notice it doesn't say He forgets, merely that He chooses not to keep a tally of all our sins. Instead, He has forgiven us and sets them aside.

Mackenzie, one of the wives from the "unsuccessful" group in Tara's research, continued to suffer in her marriage as a result of unforgiveness. "I know . . . there is this lens of stuff that I still look through," she admitted, "and I just can't seem to get around [it], and that's my deal. It's my area where I need healing." Even knowing this, she clearly remained stuck, believing that her healing would come only when her husband, Aaron, really changed. As he watched her pain and unforgiveness, he spiraled further into shame rather than recognizing the power he had to be who God created him to be, regardless of Mackenzie's unforgiveness. As a result, both lived in the powerlessness of focusing on their spouse, waiting for them to heal and change first.

Certainly, some of the harmful consequences cannot simply be left behind. If your body holds scars or irreparable damage because of what someone did to you, you will always carry that reminder with you. The beauty of forgiveness is being able to release the emotional hold the injury may have had on you. It's likely that more processing and healing will be necessary beyond forgiving, but radical acceptance and living free of the fear, shame, and control someone has had over you *is* possible. Forgiveness can be a powerful part of that journey for you.

Forgiveness Is Not Dependent on an Apology

While we must ask for God's forgiveness to *receive* His mercy, the availability of His forgiveness is not determined by our readiness to ask for it. It's there already. It's been done. We just need to receive it.

Many people believe that before they can forgive and heal, the offender must first acknowledge the wrong they have done, ask for forgiveness, and begin to change. Thankfully, this is not the case. If it were, we would be held captive and at our offenders' mercy. In some cases, our offenders are no longer in our lives. They may have died, making it impossible to confess. Others stubbornly remain in their brokenness and refuse to take ownership for their wrong behaviors or attitudes.

Forgiveness, on the other hand, is never deserved or earned. It cancels the debt rather than undoing the wrong. It can only be given sacrificially. This is true even when the offender does repent and change. If you've been harmed, the power of forgiveness is always in your hands, not only for your freedom but also, potentially, for the benefit of the offender. Yet in many cases, the offender may not even know they've been forgiven.

Forgiveness Does Not Mean Reconciliation

Before we launch into some practical steps we can take to more effectively forgive, let's explore the distinction between forgiveness and reconciliation. As noted earlier, even though reconciliation is a possible outcome of forgiveness, it is not required, nor is it always possible or even desired. For you to be personally well cared for, *forgiveness* is required, but reconciliation is optional! If reconciliation were a requirement of forgiveness, some victims would never be able to experience the full benefits and freedom of forgiveness.

Similarly, if the offender isn't interested in reconciliation, even after you offer forgiveness, this doesn't nullify your forgiveness. Remember, you have power and responsibility only for yourself. With God's help, you can walk in the freedom of leaving behind the things that have hurt you in the past and moving forward without dragging the offenses with you. You have complete power to forgive regardless of whether it is received or known.

There are also situations in which offenders continue to be dangerous. Forgiveness doesn't mean you have no boundaries. You don't need to pretend that hurtful behaviors are acceptable. You are too valuable for that! If others refuse to treat you with a level of respect reasonably due to a child of the Most High King, which you are, then it is appropriate and responsible to deny them access to you.

But what about those verses in Scripture where it sounds as if Christians are expected to accept mistreatment and anticipate persecution? For example, in the Sermon on the Mount, Jesus said, "You have heard that it was said, 'An eye for an eye and a tooth for a tooth.' But I say to you, Do not resist the one who is evil. But if anyone slaps you on the right cheek, turn to him the other also. And if anyone would sue you and take your tunic, let him have your cloak as well" (Matthew 5:38-40). But there's a difference here. Our focus is on our intimate relationships, particularly in marriage. These are people we willingly allow into our intimate, interactive space, not just random people on the street. God expects us to be highly selective about whom we allow access to our treasured hearts and the more vulnerable and valuable parts of our being. Again, "Above all else, guard your heart" (Proverbs 4:23, NIV). The kind of response Jesus spoke of is possible only when our hearts are protected, cared up, and fully dependent on God.

Reconciliation can be a wonderful possibility when forgiveness happens. It seems that God deeply desires reconciliation *for* us, just as He wants reconciliation *with* us. "If possible, so far as it depends on you, live peaceably with all" (Romans 12:18). The apostle Paul expressed this with such careful language, indicating that reconciliation is not always possible or wise. However, when both parties are willing and able to acknowledge the harm that was done and commit to changing so the offense doesn't keep happening, reconciliation is always God's heart for us.

Reconciliation can be the first step in repairing a broken relationship. It's an opportunity to grow and find deeper connections in the relationship. For safe reconciliation to happen, you may need to establish and reinforce new boundaries for how your relationship functions. All growing relationships shift and change over time. Reconciliation is not about going back to the way things were before the violation; it's often a slow process of building something fresh and new that is stronger and safer for both parties. And it doesn't require both people to have an equal say. We each have the ability and responsibility to determine when, how, whether, with whom, and under what conditions we are willing to engage.

How Rebuilding Trust Fits with Forgiveness and Reconciliation

Broken trust is a painful experience for many couples. In some ways, trust issues touch *all* relationships. Why? Because any time you trust another person, you are essentially giving them access to valuable and vulnerable areas within you. When trust is broken, those parts of your being are genuinely hurt and devalued.

Breaches in trust can be small and relatively minor, or they can be huge and devastating. For reconciliation to take place, trust must be restored. But this often creates a dilemma: Do you reopen your heart and become vulnerable again, or do you keep your heart closed and turn away from the person who hurt you? And how do you continue caring well for yourself if you reopen your heart?

For most of us, trust can be challenging because of the risks involved in being vulnerable with another flawed human being.

It's difficult when you long to be close and connected to someone who is struggling to trust you, and they remain closed and unavailable. But since the intimate bond you were created for requires an open-heart-to-open-heart connection, finding ways to trust and be trusted again becomes essential. So let's explore how we can simplify the whole business.

There are three basic commitments you and your spouse can make to establish a foundation of trust in your marriage. Each on its own adds to the safety of the relational environment. If you make all three commitments, you will become a genuinely safe person in your relationship. But if you *and* your spouse make these commitments, you'll create a truly safe and thriving relational environment.

Be Trustworthy with Yourself

This commitment requires that you recognize and respect your incredible worth and value, as well as your vulnerability. You need to be able to trust *yourself* to take care of *yourself* and not expect your spouse to ensure that your well-being is taken care of. Unless you can trust yourself to show up and make sure you're well cared for, your safety and well-being will depend on your spouse. If they get distracted and drop the ball, you're sunk. That puts way too much power over your well-being in your spouse's hands.

Did you notice in 1 Corinthians 13 that God (love) always *trusts*? How can that be when God knows we're going to break His trust? In our humanness, we simply cannot avoid it. Yet God trusts anyway!

One of our colleagues uses an illustration that may offer some perspective you can apply in your marriage. Imagine going for a hike through the woods one warm, sunny afternoon in early September. It's a beautiful day, and you're enjoying the hike until you come upon a slow-moving but fairly deep stream. As you assess the situation, you determine that the stream is at least fifteen feet across with a very deep area in the middle and about three feet deep along the bank. You also notice a wide fallen log in the water that you could use to cross the stream, and it appears that your path continues on the other side. But (in this scenario, at least) you are terrified of water because you can't swim. Would you trust the log to get you to the other side of the stream, or would you turn back?

It's likely that if you don't know how to swim, you would *not* trust the log to get you safely across the stream. The risk of falling in and drowning would be too high. If you know how to swim, you would be far more likely to trust the log (and your luck) to cross the stream, even if you're not necessarily dressed for a swim. Clearly, others have done it successfully, so even if you fall in, you know you'll be safe, though getting wet might be inconvenient.

God can always trust because He knows that even when we aren't trustworthy with Him, He is completely trustworthy with Himself. He will never forget how valuable He is, and He will never put the responsibility of caring for Himself in anyone else's hands.

We recognize, of course, that humans don't have godlike capabilities. Still, you can commit to always being trustworthy to care for your heart. God calls you to do this. Opening up and sharing the valuable parts of yourself with someone else is a privilege, even in marriage. If trust has been broken with your spouse and you are moving toward reconciliation, you need to be responsible about when and how much of yourself you share. Practice being aware of how you feel, and listen to your gut if it doesn't feel safe.

In situations when trust has been broken in the relationship, commit to showing up for yourself, setting any necessary boundaries, and using the Care Cycle to attend to any parts of yourself that need attention. When you're confident that you will consistently show up for yourself, trusting your spouse becomes radically easier.

Expect Your Spouse to Be Trustworthy with You

Closely related to being trustworthy with your own heart is expecting your spouse to treat you with respect and care. In other words, if you're going to open your heart and let your spouse in, it's completely reasonable to expect them to show themselves worthy of your trust. It's funny how we automatically have this expectation when people enter our homes. If someone came into your house and didn't wipe their muddy feet, or started breaking stuff, or rummaged through the kitchen cabinets or refrigerator without permission, you'd likely ask them to leave in short order. But do you allow your spouse, or other people, to treat you with that same degree of carelessness and disrespect and say nothing about it?

This is different from expecting them to care for your well-being. Remember, self-care is your responsibility alone. Expecting your spouse to be trustworthy is more about establishing and maintaining boundaries regarding how you expect to be treated and under what conditions you will grant access to your inner self. It also includes being clear about what you will do when your spouse (or anyone else) becomes careless and forgets how precious, valuable, and vulnerable your heart really is. That will happen. (Later in the book, we share some detailed steps for setting healthy and righteous boundaries.)

For now, when your spouse forgets to treat you with care, you can simply pull back and respectfully inform them that access to your heart is a special privilege, by invitation only, and you won't remain in their presence if they continue to treat you poorly. Your spouse and other people who want access to your heart need to prove they are worthy of your trust. You don't owe them your trust; it is earned and must be maintained through respectful, honoring behavior. When they show themselves trustworthy, access can be granted again.

When you expect others to be worthy of your trust by treating you with respect and honor, you will gain self-confidence and begin to trust yourself more. Then, even if your spouse becomes careless and forgets how valuable you are, *you will never forget*!

Commit to Being Trustworthy with Your Spouse

In the same way, you must also be trustworthy with your spouse's heart. When your spouse grants you access to their innermost self, it is just as special a privilege. You want to do everything in your power to avoid hurting, devaluing, disrespecting, or dishonoring them. A trustworthy person recognizes that no one owes them trust. Your power lies in focusing on being as worthy of your spouse's trust as possible and humbly allowing your spouse to determine the extent to which they feel safe trusting you.

‡

Now pause and think about the potential significance of these three commitments to your marriage; being trustworthy with yourself, expecting your spouse to be trustworthy with you, and being trustworthy with your spouse. As we pointed out earlier, when you make all three commitments, you will be a genuinely safe person in your relationship. But when *both* of you commit to being trustworthy in all three areas, your relational environment, and your marriage, will become a genuinely safe haven—a sanctuary each of you can run to.

Steps to Forgiveness

Now that we have a framework for what forgiveness is and isn't and have teased apart the concepts of reconciliation and trust, we're ready to work through a practical model of forgiveness, based on a list Dr. Tat-Ying Wong created.[3] As you reflect on each of the following steps, you may find it helpful to journal your responses to the activities and questions.

Step 1: Acknowledge the Hurt

To effectively forgive someone, it is important to fully acknowledge what happened. In this step, write out all the ways you were hurt. Include the hurtful words, attitudes, and behaviors of the person who harmed you.

Step 2: Acknowledge the Feelings and Consequences of the Hurt and Rate Them

Dig deeper and explore the feelings you've experienced as a result of what happened. In addition, consider other consequences, including any financial, physical, relational, spiritual, and social damage you sustained. Some people find it helpful to rate the intensity of these consequences on a scale of 1 to 10. This can give you a sense of validation that there are authentic reasons why it has been hard to forgive. As you work through these first two steps, you may find yourself beginning to release the pain.

Step 3: Discover the Cause of the Hurt

The following ten factors can help you uncover the cause of the hurt you experienced. As you explore these areas and answer the corresponding questions, consider other related factors that may be at the root of your pain. Some of these factors relate to what the other person has done, and others relate to what might have contributed to your vulnerability to being hurt in this way.

- *Unmet needs.* Were any of my normal human needs unmet, including the need for love, respect, significance, value, acceptance, forgiveness, fairness, security, safety, trust, purpose, meaning, autonomy, and agency?
- *Broken expectations.* Did I have unmet expectations related to myself, others, relationships, results, and even consequences?
- *Violated rights.* Were my individual rights violated, such as the right to be loved, respected, and valued; the right to have choices, opinions, and my own feelings; or the right to equality and fairness?
- *Boundary intrusions.* Was I required to take responsibility for or suffer the consequences of someone else's choices, actions, feelings, or beliefs?
- *Broken rules.* Were the rules I live by broken? Examples include spoken and unspoken rules about how people should behave, communicate, and handle conflict; roles and responsibilities; or rights and privileges.
- *Negative thoughts.* Did any negative thought patterns contribute to my being hurt, such as black-or-white thinking, exaggerating, using negative filters, discounting positives, catastrophizing, "shoulding" people, mind reading, holding double standards, or labeling?
- *Distorted, unhealthy beliefs.* Did any unhealthy or mistaken beliefs about people, God, and relationships contribute to my being hurt?
- *Value and priority conflicts.* Were my personal values or priorities disrespected or compromised in any way?
- *Unhealthy attitudes.* Did any unhealthy attitudes set me up for being hurt? Examples include entitlement, perfectionism, pride, self-centeredness, dependency, passiveness, aggressiveness, victim mentality, and helplessness.

- *Unhelpful perspectives.* Did any rigid, limiting, or
  constraining perspectives contribute to my being hurt?

Step 4: Deal with and Resolve the Cause of the Hurt

Review the previous ten factors and prayerfully consider how to
care for yourself as you seek to address what caused the hurt. In
some cases, you may find healthier ways to get your needs met or
reinforce boundaries that are defective or deficient. Also be open
to God's conviction and redirection. He may draw your attention
to thinking patterns, beliefs, attitudes, and actions He wants to
change so they're more in line with the person of integrity He
created you to be. Or He may ask you to reexamine areas of your
life or lay something down for His higher purposes. If you haven't
already, consider the humanity and brokenness of your offender
and take some time remembering how much Jesus paid for your
forgiveness. Wrestle with Him over these things, trusting that any
correction or redirection is for your benefit and freedom.

Step 5: Decide to Forgive

We have now reached the point of decision. Take some time to
consider the pros and cons of forgiving the person who hurt you.
Be honest and thoughtful during this process, and ask the Lord
to help you. Being open and honest with yourself about what
happened may reveal other areas that need care, attention, or correction, including fears or beliefs. This step is solely about your
freedom and healing.

Step 6: Offer Forgiveness

Where possible, and only if it's safe, look for ways to make it easy
for your offender to receive your forgiveness. You are offering an
undeserved gift to this person, so it's important to offer it without

any bitterness, arrogance, or contempt. If you're struggling with these feelings, consider repeating these steps or working through the Care Cycle again until you're ready to offer forgiveness with grace and gentleness.

‡

Through this process of forgiveness, you release the offender and the offense, as well as your attempts to control the situation that led to the hurt you experienced. You also surrender justice to the Lord. He will take care of it. You can confidently step into freedom from holding on to your pain and reliving the violation. God doesn't want you to live in that place. Forgiveness also frees you to reopen the doors of your heart fully to God so that He can heal and restore you. Another possible result of forgiveness is moving toward reconciliation when, and if, it is safe and wise to do so.

Trust will always be a vacillating thing. But as you learn to be trustworthy with your own heart, you can safely protect it if you decide to pursue reconciliation, and pull back if your heart feels unsafe. In most cases, you'll find that reconciliation will strengthen your relationship and take you to deeper levels of connection and intimacy.

Throughout part 1 of this book, we have been encouraging you to practice personal responsibility and self-care in your personal life and your relationship with your spouse. Next, we'll explore how everything we've discussed thus far can empower you to have a fulfilling and deeply satisfying marriage. From a place of safety and being cared up, you are now ready to engage your spouse in the shared garden of your relationship with openness and vulnerability, knowing you can trust yourself to stay safe. As both of you show up in this way for each other, the possibilities for intimacy, connection, and enjoyment in your marriage are endless!

Part 2

8

BEING GOOD
TOGETHER

UP UNTIL NOW, we have focused primarily on getting *you* on course individually, positioning you to be whole and healthy and ready for an amazing adventure with your spouse and God. This increases the likelihood that the deeper longings of your heart will be satisfied so that you can be your best self in your marriage and fulfill your purpose in this world. From that more empowered place, you can connect to God, better understand His plan for your life, and turn your attention to building a stronger relationship with your spouse. These next chapters, then, are about how to be really good *together*.

As much as we want you to be healthy and fulfilled personally, if that is all you accomplish, your marriage will probably feel like two people traveling down parallel tracks that never meet. But that's not the recipe for a satisfying *relationship*. For your marriage to really thrive, how you and your spouse do "us" has to be good too! Remember, our definition of a great marriage is nothing less than two people *thrilled* with their relationship *and* the direction it is heading!

Getting there won't always be pretty. Some days you'll celebrate your victories, other days you'll face your demons and fight your common enemies, and sometimes you'll just catch your breath, relax, and be still. Life together as a married couple in the real world is *not* about "happily ever after." That's just for fairy tales! In the real world, married life is a long journey, and the partner you've chosen will be with you through sickness and health, for better or worse, till death do you part. There are many moments of happiness along the way, and we want to help you increase those moments. There are also many moments and seasons in marriage when "happy" is hard to find. Those are the times you really need a friendship you can count on!

Where It All Fits, What It All Means

To establish some practical ways you can be good together and make your marriage great, let's revisit the Healthy Marriage Model from chapter 2. Ideally, you and your spouse have already embraced the responsibility of caring for yourselves individually. Perfection isn't required, merely owning full responsibility. Each of you will heal and grow throughout your lifetimes, assuming you're functioning as responsible adults and not codependently looking to your spouse to fill you or complete you—or blaming your spouse for not meeting your wants and needs. Accepting the job of caring for yourself leads to feeling more empowered and safe in your own skin. The benefit relationally is a safe environment that comes from operating responsibly, resisting the blame game, and managing yourself well so you can keep bringing your best self to the relationship.

You have no control over your spouse or whether they do their part, but when you do yours, you greatly increase the odds of your marriage improving over time. Only *you* are responsible for how you show up. God is expecting you to care well for His precious child.

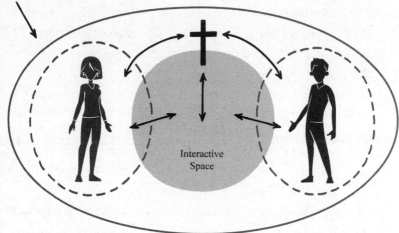

Covenant Marriage Boundary

Interactive Space

As our diagram shows, in a healthy marriage, two responsible adults join together in a covenant, making commitments to each other for the purpose of creating a safe environment. In this space, you and your spouse can allow yourselves to be known, even as you're learning more about yourselves as individuals. It's a place where you can face life's challenges together and enjoy the benefits of a truly intimate union!

When done well and wisely, both of you will work diligently to make sure your interactive space is a haven where you can rest, recharge, and connect. If you don't want to find yourself hanging out there alone, take the time to understand what will make this a space your spouse loves to join you in. When your interactive space becomes a place both of you are eager to return to, it will be your sanctuary, the safest place in the world. One of our colleagues calls it his "sunny meadow." It's his favorite place to relax, play, and reconnect, so he can bring his best self to the Lord and the world.

In this safe and intimate sanctuary, each of you are free not only to be naked and unashamed (Genesis 2:25) but also to be naked and *unafraid*!

Safe and Secure . . . with Boundaries

As we have reiterated throughout this book, feeling safe together is the foundation of a great marriage. The kind of safety we're talking about goes far beyond physical safety. It includes our minds, emotions, and spirits too. If you look at the Healthy Marriage Model, you'll notice that all the circles represent boundaries. For a marriage to be healthy and safe, those boundaries must be respected and maintained.

I (Bob) am responsible for me and everything within me. My identity, my heart, my body, and every other aspect of my being must be protected and attended to. Boundaries establish lines of responsibility that should help protect what is within me. They also help distinguish what is me and what is not me, as well as what is my responsibility and what is not mine.

Early in our marriage, it was a big surprise when I figured out that Jenni's personal boundaries needed to be completely honored and supported. That meant I entered only when invited, and I needed to leave promptly and respectfully when asked. I'd always believed that when we got married, there would be no more boundaries between us. Everything that was mine would be ours, and everything that was Jenni's would be ours as well.

But God helped me see that in a truly healthy marriage, boundaries must exist. Jenni is fully responsible before God for the well-being and upkeep of the temple she occupies. When I violate her boundaries, I am damaging and devaluing God's treasure—His daughter—and she is responsible for ensuring that doesn't happen, even in our marriage. As Jenni's husband, it's critical that I respect her boundaries.

But I was slow to see it. Remember how I would come to Jenni when I was upset about something she did and tell her what I wanted her to do differently next time? She always hated those conversations! But one day she did something that really caught me off guard. When I approached her wanting to talk and started laying out my case for what she should change that would be more to my liking, she simply said no and then walked away. Unaware of how firm her response was, I followed her from room to room, continuing to present my case. Finally she ended up in the bedroom, where she forcefully shut and locked the door.

I actually saw that as an advantage, since I now had a captive audience. Figuring I might as well get comfortable, I sat down outside the door and kept up my rationalized rant until . . . I heard the car start outside. Looking out the front window, I realized that Jenni had climbed out the bedroom window and was now making her escape. I was fit to be tied! I thought, *She doesn't care about me or our marriage, and she obviously doesn't care about God!* I couldn't have been more self-righteous—and deceived.

At some point, I saw how wrong I was on virtually all counts. I'd told myself that my goals were in the best interests of our marriage. In reality, *self-interest* was my deeper objective. Creating a safe place for Jenni in our relationship wasn't in the equation.

That interactive space in your marriage, your supposed sanctuary, is never a safe place until you and your spouse feel completely safe to *leave*. You can't feel safe to say yes until you feel free to say no without fearing you'll regret it. Unfortunately, I provided none of that for Jenni at the time. I'd made our interactive space feel very unsafe for her, and she had every reason to "get out of Dodge" until I came to my senses.

Responsibility, Freedom, Peace, and Power

Freedom, peace, and power—who doesn't want those things? But where does responsibility fit in? At the beginning of the list, of course! Yet many people, often adolescents, think of freedom as freedom *from* responsibility. To them, freedom means "going to the beach without a care in the world," "being able to do anything I want, whenever I want," "nobody telling me what to do," and so on. But freedom is not the absence of responsibility. Freedom and responsibility are two sides of the same coin. You are truly free only in direct proportion to the degree of personal responsibility you accept.

If you want a safe place to live, food on the table, and a good life, you need to work, save for the future, and attend to all areas of your well-being. In other words, you need to live as a responsible adult. Otherwise, your health and well-being are, at best, determined by others or, at worst, not attended to at all. The more you embrace personal responsibility, the more you will be able to positively influence ultimate outcomes.

The same is true for peace. Remember the Serenity Prayer? "God, grant me the serenity to accept the things I cannot change, the courage to change the things I can, and the wisdom to know the difference."[1] Responsibility is linked to peace in a different way than it is to freedom. Having real peace depends more on understanding what you're responsible for, recognizing what you're not responsible for, and deciding to take on only the responsibilities in your own yard.

And what about power? Hopefully by now it's easy to see that true personal power is integrally tied to responsibility. I (Bob) have *righteous power* in the areas I am responsible for. But I would have to become manipulative and controlling to gain a degree of *undeserved power* in the areas I'm not responsible for.

These distinctions are crucial in relationships. Since problems in marriage are regularly the result of misplaced responsibilities, we developed something we call *the law of personal responsibility*. It goes like this:

> *I am fully responsible for my own thoughts, feelings, beliefs, and behavior.*
> *I have absolutely no responsibility for others' thoughts, feelings, beliefs, and behavior.*
> *In a relationship, I can influence others' thoughts, feelings, beliefs, and behaviors, but I do not determine them.*

For all our relationships to be healthy, we need to stay within the lines of this law. This is especially true in marriage, where so many temptations, wayward beliefs, and cultural expectations can confuse us and send us down a wrong path. It's natural that we want to do everything within our power to exert a positive influence in our marriages and our spouses' lives. But we must be careful not to cross the line and attempt to control outcomes by taking responsibility for things that aren't ours to take.

This can become confusing and complicated if you're married to a spouse who abdicates personal responsibility. These challenges are real, and the consequences can be detrimental to you and your family. But you must continually remind yourself that you are responsible only for your own well-being and self-care. In such circumstances, the Care Cycle is an invaluable asset. If your situation is more extreme, you may need to take stronger measures. Through it all, remain in prayerful communication with the Lord, trusting in His guidance. In situations where hearing from God is difficult and you feel overwhelmed, remember that His voice—His wisdom, love, and truth—can often be heard through a wise and trusted friend or counselor.

Embracing your God-directed responsibility to care for yourself is essential if you want to experience the maximum amount of freedom, peace, and power available to you. That's how you can equip yourself to handle life's unexpected curveballs and seize the opportunities that come your way.

Enjoying the Intimate Adventure

Back in chapter 3, we briefly discussed getting to know yourself and your spouse better over time, embracing the adventure of knowing and being known. We explored how an attitude of curiosity and fascination is central to a marriage filled with romance and passion. That means sharing what each of you is learning about yourself, God, your spouse, relationships, and life in general. There is always something new and exciting to discuss when you're curious. So with that as a starting point, we want to share what we consider the most powerful relationship-building skill: learning to formulate and ask great questions.

Pretty underwhelming, right? But we're serious. We know of no more effective way to demonstrate real interest in another person than being curious enough to ask them thoughtful questions to know them better. Have you ever met someone who finds you fascinating and hangs on your every word? Their attention is focused on you, as if you're the most important person in the world! It's as if they're saying, "I care about you so much, I just want to know you—how you feel, what you want, and what matters to you."

Questions drive the journey of discovery—but all questions are not created equal. Better questions yield better results. This is the basis of any well-executed scientific investigation. Scientists start with a question that needs to be answered. This gets translated into a hypothesis, which scientists set out to examine and test. What they learn from their research informs and changes the questions they're asking, which encourages them to look deeper or shift their focus in a different direction to see what they can find. Some of the greatest discoveries in history were made when explorers allowed questions to guide their journeys.

God also makes a big deal about asking questions. He instructs His children to "seek first the kingdom of God and his righteousness, and all these things will be added to you" (Matthew 6:33). In fact, He implores us to "ask, and it will be given to you; seek, and you will find; knock, and it will be opened to you. For everyone who asks receives, and the one who seeks finds, and to the one who knocks it will be opened" (Matthew 7:7-8). As seekers, we are to be curious about our relationship with God and His Kingdom, always asking questions and looking for answers.

Some years ago, I (Bob) wrote a book called *Finding Ever After*, in which I offered four tips to help couples formulate good questions and hone their quest of discovery in marriage.[2] I present these tips again here, with updated commentary:

1. *Allow your curiosity to create questions.* This a great place to start. If you are genuinely interested in something, questions will naturally emerge. You'll begin asking questions like "I wonder if . . ." or "I wonder how . . ." or "I wonder why . . ." When your interest is authentic, wanting to explore something further doesn't require much effort. Finding your spouse intriguing will generate lots of great questions too. If you have the interest but can't think of good questions to ask, search the internet for lists of questions you can draw from. You'll find an amazing abundance of them online! These questions can enhance any date with your spouse.

2. *Embrace confusion.* Many people are afraid of (or fundamentally averse to) confusion. Not knowing something feels uncomfortable and is often seen as a lack of intelligence. In reality, feeling uncertain and confused can be an amazing relational asset. When we're not afraid of how we're being perceived, questions naturally bubble up. At times, we find our spouses baffling because they're so different from us. When something Vince does or says or thinks confuses me (Tara), it can put me off, and I may judge or reject it. But when I choose to lean in without judgment and seek instead to understand, I seize an opportunity to express interest and fascination in someone I love who is so different from me. What I often discover is powerfully new and fresh!

3. *See the value of unanswered questions.* When most of us ask questions, we typically want instant answers. Unanswered questions just hanging out there feel like dangling loose ends—awkward and incomplete. However, when we allow important questions to focus our attention on figuring

things out relationally, they can help us stay engaged with our spouses. If you're driven by fascination and interest, unanswered questions and unresolved issues don't have to put you off. I (Bob) have many unanswered questions about God, and I figure that many of them won't be answered until I meet Him face-to-face in heaven. But that just keeps me intrigued. There are also a bunch of things about Jenni that I still don't get. And fortunately, by God's grace, I still have time to continue getting to know her. I actually hope I never learn all the answers to my questions about her. Boredom would set in, and I want my marriage to remain filled with curiosity, romance, and passion!

4. *Make use of empathy.* Empathy is putting yourself in your spouse's shoes and trying to see the world as they see and experience it. Often this includes feeling *with* someone. The goal is to communicate that you care enough to *want* to see what they see and feel what they feel, and then *actually* seeing and feeling things their way. When done well, empathy produces a deep feeling of connection and bonding as you and your spouse experience each other's point of view. To accomplish this, sensitive and thoughtful questions are gold. Asking your spouse what an experience was like for them emotionally, or how they see a situation, or what they most want in a given moment can deepen your connection and help them feel truly cared for.

Feeling Alive Together

We have made the case that your marriage can be filled with romance, passion, and adventure when you embrace the journey of getting to know each other more deeply. We've also explored the importance of including things in your life that make you feel truly alive. As you and your spouse learn and grow together, you create a launching pad from which to experience some of the best things life has to offer. Being good together means including activities and experiences in your marriage that can take your growing friendship to the next level.

Life is often quite serious, yet God created humans with an incredible capacity to enjoy life. Many of us have a wonderful sense of humor, with an ability to laugh until our sides ache. We can play hard, turning almost anything into a game or activity that delights our souls. We can explore nature and stretch our physical limits in ways that give us an amazing sense of accomplishment. We can invest ourselves in activities that change lives and advance the Kingdom of God. When you add these elements to a relationship you've built on a foundation of safety, love, and trust, the adventure of marriage becomes a source of awe and wonder.

One of my (Bob's) daughters is married to a race-car driver. He's driven in races around the world, and when he was younger, he drove professionally on Subaru's Rally Team. He's still passionate about the sport and looks for opportunities to race whenever he can. My daughter supports his passion, frequently attending races and participating in events. She shares his love of cars and has become quite knowledgeable herself. My son-in-law is great at making my daughter feel involved and included, and the two have had some amazing adventures together at racing events.

They also seek out adventures where they can be mutually active. For example, they love riding bikes together, but they've become serious enough about cycling that they often train separately. Riding bikes has become one of many points of connection in their marriage. Even when life is stressing them out, and they don't really feel like riding, they get back on their bikes, and a few miles down the road, the endorphins start flowing, the fresh air replenishes their brains, and they find themselves decompressing, smiling together, and feeling reconnected.

Other ways to play together as a couple can include something as simple as regular game nights. Whatever the activity, the key is having fun together. It can be something just the two of you enjoy, or it can include family and friends. As long as the end result is feeling more alive and connected as a couple, it works.

Vince and I (Tara) love traveling together and experiencing new places. When we travel, we look for adventurous things to do that are out of the ordinary, such as climbing a rock face with a *via ferrata* or hiking to a secluded chapel high above a medieval village. These adventures breathe life into our marriage as nothing else can.

In chapter 3, we explored the importance of romance and adventure in your relationship, so flip back to that chapter if you need a refresher. We encourage you to search high and low for activities you can enjoy as a couple that will breathe life and passion into your marriage.

Finding Purpose Together

As we have said several times, we were all created on purpose for a purpose. We can't emphasize enough the importance of becoming who God created you to be and doing what He designed you to do. That applies in marriage as well! Fulfilling your purpose as a couple is just as important as it is individually. But without an intentional focus, you can miss opportunities to find your purpose together.

God called me (Bob) to help couples in marital crisis repair and restore their marriages. Jenni, however, is not a therapist and doesn't join me in that work. God has a different purpose for her life. But as a couple, we look for ways we can serve Christ together. For more than forty years, we have had many opportunities to fulfill our purpose on this journey together. In earlier seasons of our marriage, we invested in the next generation by raising our kids and preparing them to find their respective places in God's plan. We also served together in different ways at church and in other contexts. At times I've jumped into something Jenni felt called to do, and she has joined me in something God has led me to do. Today we lead a Life Group and speak together publicly. Recently we even served together as parking attendants for a massive church event. We looked great in our reflective vests waving our light wands! Every one of these investments has been rich and meaningful because we allowed our Lord to lead us as a couple and use us for His purposes—including parking cars!

The key to finding your purpose together is seeking God's direction and allowing Him to lead you. One of the best and most important ways to find your purpose is praying *together*. Unfortunately, it's not a regular practice in many marriages today. Prayer is simply communicating with your heavenly Father. He wants to spend time with you and guide you to opportunities to join Him as a couple in what He's doing in the world.

Prayer is such a deeply personal experience that praying aloud as a couple can feel uncomfortable, awkward, and vulnerable at first. Keep in mind that praying with your spouse is an extremely intimate interaction that happens within the interactive space of your marriage. To share the deepest, most vulnerable parts of yourselves in prayer, you both need to feel safe. Like other interactions in this space, praying together requires the same commitment to making this a sanctuary where you can go to find spiritual renewal and direction as a couple. Pursuing God together is critical for a Christian marriage to be all it's meant to be. Without that key component, something will always be missing! To feel good seeking God together, leave room for individual differences in the ways you express yourselves in prayer. Spend extra time making sure you feel safe and comfortable enough with each other spiritually so you can enter God's presence together with open hearts and no reservations!

Relational Balance

In chapter 6, we focused on the importance of finding balance in your personal life. Here, we'll briefly discuss how that plays out relationally in marriage. Figuring out how to balance the various aspects of your marriage so both of you feel good about it can be quite a feat. But it's a goal worth pursuing.

What constitutes balance in a marriage can vary from couple to couple, and even from spouse to spouse. For instance, some couples work together, and some work separately. In some marriages, one spouse works from home, while the other spouse works at an office or travels out of town. Some spouses receive a paycheck, and others contribute to the family in ways that don't generate direct income. What feels like balance to one couple in their unique situation won't necessarily apply to other couples.

Here are some time-related aspects of everyday life that couples typically need to balance:

- time together versus time apart
- time managing the house and family versus time relaxing and playing
- time invested in team-oriented activities versus time spent on personal interests
- time invested in the marriage versus time invested in the children and family

All these, and more, reflect essential elements of personal and relational well-being. However, you and your spouse may value each element differently. What's most important is that you and your spouse clarify which elements matter most to each of you personally and relationally; then work together to create relational balance in those areas.

In the following chapters, we will equip you with two powerful tools that can help you and your spouse sort out what is most important to each of you; discuss it all in a safe, respectful, and affirming way; and come up with solutions and strategies both of you feel great about. Remember, a great marriage is nothing less than two people *thrilled* with their relationship and the direction it is heading!

9

SPEAKING
FROM THE HEART

PLENTY OF VERBAL AND NONVERBAL COMMUNICATION takes place in a marriage. But all too often that communication is neither effective nor satisfying. Poor communication may be the most common relational challenge married couples encounter. To create a marriage that both spouses are thrilled with, clear communication is essential, especially when strong feelings are involved. Under stressful and emotional circumstances, poor communication leaves couples disappointed and frustrated, feeling like two disconnected people traveling down parallel tracks that never reconnect.

Now we'll turn our attention to some simple communication tools you and your spouse can use to build open, vulnerable, and safe connections through effective and meaningful conversations. These tools are like guardrails that will help you keep important conversations securely on the road so you'll arrive safely at your desired destination. We think you'll find that learning these methods will pay big dividends in your marriage. When done well, each of you will feel heard, understood, and mutually empowered to love well. This is where your communication can really shine!

As we emphasized earlier, safety is crucial for establishing openness and vulnerability. It also sets up opportunities to connect in meaningful ways with your spouse. The best communication between a husband and wife always happens in a safe, relational interactive space. When you enter that space cared up and filled up as individuals, it's so much easier to be accepting and curious about each other. From there, as two imperfect people uniquely created and loved by God, you can fully embrace the journey of getting to know each other in deeper ways. This is *real* intimacy! Differences are no longer the enemy; they are the spice that makes life interesting. We can celebrate and fully utilize them as God intended.

When I (Tara) married Vince, I wasn't very good at money management. Though I made a fairly good living for a young adult, I always seemed to live paycheck to paycheck. I not only carried debt from graduate school into my marriage; I also didn't think much about savings. In all honesty, I realized there were better ways to handle my finances, but I didn't know what to do differently. Vince, however, is amazing with finances, so we had several conversations about money management, and he helped me learn how to live within a budget. I love the freedom that living within our means now brings us!

Being a good and grateful steward of God's resources was a priority for me, but at the time, Vince wasn't tithing. After some great conversations about it, he got on board with regular, generous giving. Vince and I love reviewing how much we've been able to give over the years because of how we manage our finances. Handled well, our differences have blessed both of us. And looking back, we recognize that safe and effective communication made it possible.

We have spent years studying what makes the biggest difference in communication among couples. So we weren't surprised to discover that couples who reported the most satisfaction in marriage were good communicators. What made the difference? These couples knew *how* and *when* to use the two key communication tools we'll be sharing with you in this chapter and the next. As with any job, using the wrong tool for the task at hand can set you up for failure. And if either of you is using the wrong communication tool, you will likely have a dissatisfying conversation.

The first tool we'll lay out in this chapter is *Heart Talk*, which focuses on feelings and is useful for connection, intimacy, and emotional understanding between you and your spouse. Then in the next chapter, we'll talk about the second tool: *Work Talk*. This tool focuses on problem-solving and is useful for managing differences and conflict in your marriage.

Communication between you and your spouse can improve quickly when both tools are understood, when you're both clear about when and how to use each one, and when you make sure you're both using the same tool. And since you'll need to master the skills involved, a little practice will ensure maximum success and satisfaction.

Heart Talk

We recommend the Heart Talk tool for staying connected with your spouse and making meaningful investments in your marriage. Its simplicity and openness will help you develop a safe and secure interactive space while also making room for your spicy differences.

As the name suggests, Heart Talk enables you and your spouse to truly hear each other's deeper feelings. Perhaps more importantly, it also allows those feelings to matter. A truly satisfying marriage makes room for each spouse's deeper feelings to be present and accounted for. You need to share emotions verbally with each other; otherwise, you will be left to guess or assume what the other person is feeling—that's rarely a safe or reliable system! This is especially true if you've been married for some time. Since you're always in the process of growing, Heart Talk ensures that there is room to keep learning about each other so you can enjoy the journey *together*.

Heart Talk is a little like looking through a window into another person's soul. If your desire is to really know your spouse, Heart Talk will give you a powerful opportunity to see the world, your circumstances, and even yourself from their perspective. As you learn how unique your spouse is, God's incredible creativity will fill you with awe. You'll also discover the giftings your spouse possesses that differ from your own. Indeed, seeing the world through the eyes and experiences of another person is one of the best opportunities for personal growth.

Please note that Heart Talk is not intended to solve problems. As important as it is to "fix" the issues in your marriage, this is not the tool for that purpose. (We'll get to that tool in the next chapter.) Heart Talk is about forging the intimate bond that becomes the foundation of real friends, trusted lovers, and skillful teammates.

We also don't intend for you and your spouse to start your communication journey in the deepest waters of the emotional pool. Developing safety and security in marriage takes time and effort. Heart Talk is a pathway to get you there.

Remember that building your interactive space—your

sanctuary—is possible only when you and your spouse are cared up or at least making solid progress toward personal responsibility and self-care. To construct a great marriage and a satisfying relational environment, it helps if you have something to contribute. If you're feeling compromised or neglected emotionally, spiritually, physically, or mentally (ESPM), you're not likely to show up caring and curious about your differences.

For instance, I (Tara) know that when I'm tired, I'm not as interested in hearing Vince's detailed thought processes. I can become impatient or distracted, especially if I'd rather be reading or relaxing. That typically doesn't feel safe for Vince and can make it harder for him to share, even when I finally get myself cared up and ready. If we're discussing anything of great importance, I'm unlikely to be trustworthy with his heart if I'm not feeling well cared for myself. But when I'm cared up, I can more easily give my full attention to Vince. Even though he sees the world quite differently than I do, I can be genuinely curious to see what he sees, and the differences in how he looks at things are fascinating to me.

Heart Talk is a versatile tool that can make even hard topics easier and safer to discuss. What's more, it eliminates taboo topics in a marriage. Obviously, some topics will be more emotionally charged for each of you, but when you know there is a safe, structured way to communicate that values both the speaker and the listener, then connection is possible even if the conversations are difficult. When Heart Talk is done well, hard topics can create some of the most rewarding connections. The confidence that comes from knowing that both of you are committed to and skilled at managing emotionally charged topics can make you feel almost invincible. Together, you can overcome any issue!

How Heart Talk Works

As with any new skill you learn, you may feel a bit awkward and uncomfortable with Heart Talk at first. We get that. But with practice, this tool will help you achieve the deeper connection you long for. For added clarity and safety, we recommend that you closely follow the Heart Talk structure to begin with. Then as you become more confident in your ability to safely and effectively discuss emotionally charged topics, you and your spouse can customize the process to best fit your personalities and styles.

Before we get into the details, let's set the ideal environment for Heart Talk. There are only three steps in the process, and they are basically the same for each person. Because Heart Talk is about matters of the heart, and God has charged each of you to carefully guard your own heart (Proverbs 4:23), we like to use the ICU acronym for these steps. Hopefully, this brings to mind an intensive care unit in a hospital. In most hospital wards, one or two nurses may care for several patients, but in an ICU, one nurse is dedicated to caring for one or two patients at a time, and special attention is given to keeping the environment quiet and calm.

Your Heart Talk goal is to create a marital ICU, a safe interactive space where your hearts are well cared for. We want both of you to have complete confidence that you can share your most vulnerable personal information with each other without any regrets.

The most basic setup for Heart Talk may at first appear ridiculously obvious. There are two distinct roles: a speaker and a listener. Since the goal is making sure that each spouse's feelings are heard, understood, and cared for, neither spouse's emotions can be viewed as more important than the other's, nor can they be overlooked, ignored, or judged. In reality, many communication breakdowns occur when both parties are trying to be heard at the same time (two simultaneous speakers and no listener), or no one is really listening (which includes listening for the purpose of pointing out how wrong your spouse's thoughts or feelings are). Successful Heart Talk requires you and your spouse to take turns being the complete focus of attention. And each role has distinctly different expectations and responsibilities. The basic Heart Talk structure is as follows:

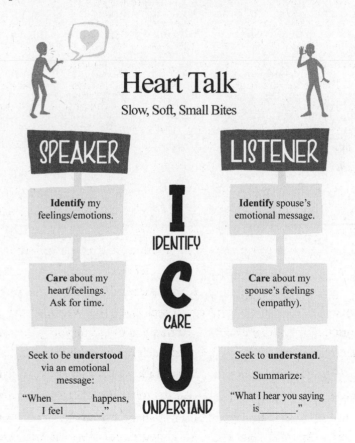

Heart Talk
Slow, Soft, Small Bites

SPEAKER		LISTENER
Identify my feelings/emotions.	**I** — IDENTIFY	**Identify** spouse's emotional message.
Care about my heart/feelings. Ask for time.	**C** — CARE	**Care** about my spouse's feelings (empathy).
Seek to be **understood** via an emotional message: "When _____ happens, I feel _____."	**U** — UNDERSTAND	Seek to **understand**. Summarize: "What I hear you saying is _____."

The Speaker Role

When you enter into a heart talk as the speaker, you share feelings you believe would be valuable or useful for your spouse to know about. Your primary job is to attempt to identify what you're feeling and then find ways to clearly communicate that feeling to your spouse. This opens the door for an intimate encounter. You are sharing your heart, so you need to be careful with it. Ultimately, it is always your responsibility to do what you can to keep it safe, even during heart talks.

Typically, as the speaker, you will complete the Identify and Care steps before you share with your spouse. As you think about what you want to share, identify the feelings, longings, fears, and desires you would like your spouse to know about. Early on, it may be helpful to write out the specific words that best capture what is going on inside you. This helps focus your message on your feelings, not on what your spouse did or said, or your perception of what happened.

While not essential, the Care Cycle can be a great way to explore your feelings. The five As of the cycle—Aware, Accept, Allow, Attend, and Act—can often lead to a better personal understanding of your feelings. This can help you communicate them clearly to your spouse, increasing the likelihood of being heard and understood. When your feelings have been triggered, learning more about yourself and the roots of those triggers can be meaningful things to share with your spouse and will help them know you better.

The Care step includes deciding that your feelings matter enough to you to spend a few minutes caring for them as you prepare to give your spouse an opportunity to care about them too. If you really want to be heard and understood, it makes good sense to think of how to construct your heart message in a way that will make sense to your spouse. Also be mindful of how you can best present your message so it won't feel to your spouse like an attack, blame, or criticism. This will increase the likelihood that they will receive it without getting defensive. The key is to keep your message focused on *you* and *your feelings*. Steer clear of opinions or beliefs about your spouse or their behavior.

An important part of caring for your heart is making sure that before you share anything, your spouse is open and available to enter a conversation. This means asking your spouse if they are ready and interested in being a listener. Much is required of listeners in a heart talk, so you need to give your spouse the option to not participate if they aren't prepared to take on that role. If they aren't open or available, sharing your heart message is careless and irresponsible. Caring for yourself means sharing your feelings only when your spouse is ready and willing to handle the information with care.

If your spouse says no, then you can either agree on another time that would work for both of you or allow your spouse to let you know when they're ready. This doesn't mean your spouse "dodged a bullet" and got out of having that talk. Remember, for your marriage to thrive, you need to have safe heart-to-heart conversations. That's the only way to build intimacy. If your spouse isn't ready for a heart talk, they will need to be intentional about getting cared up enough to have the conversation.

People frequently ask us, "What if my spouse is *never* ready for a heart talk?" We hope that won't be the case in your marriage, but it's always a possibility. Obviously, if one spouse isn't willing to engage emotionally, the ability to connect heart to heart will be virtually eliminated. It also communicates that they really don't want to know their spouse in a deeper way. That doesn't mean the marriage is somehow invalid or that connecting in other ways isn't possible. But it can be disappointing or even heartbreaking for the spouse who is seeking an intimate bond. However, every individual has a God-given right to say no, and doing your part to make the environment safe in your marriage must include giving your spouse the freedom to decline an invitation to talk on a deeper level. Your spouse's right to decline a heart talk is one big reason why we emphasize being cared up prior to requesting one.

If your spouse isn't open to emotional intimacy, you are not alone. My (Tara's) marriage often feels like that, though I choose to focus on other ways Vince loves me and cares about me. At this point, he simply isn't at a place where he wants to hear about or connect with my feelings very often. It seems as if that would be a totally different language for him, and I don't want him to feel like he is failing me if he can't do this well.

Interestingly, as I've pulled back and not required him to listen to my feelings or held it against him, I've found that he is more able to engage in this way on occasion. While we may not go as deep as I might like, I fully appreciate, enjoy, and even savor the moments when we do engage on an emotional level. The rest of the time, I've learned to wait well, care for my own heart, and draw deeper into a powerful intimacy with God that I don't think I would have sought out if Vince had been more available from the start. As a result, I've discovered the God-given power I have at my disposal.

Once you've identified your feelings and taken time to care for them, you're ready for the third step: *seeking to be understood*. This is where you share your heart message with your spouse. To help keep your message focused on your feelings, we recommend structuring your statements like this: "When x happened, I felt/I feared/I longed for . . ." The first part of your message establishes the context (what happened), but the main part expresses the feeling. You could also say it this way: "When I think of x, I feel/I fear/I long for . . ." It's always important to keep the context ("When I think of . . .")

short and focused on your heart message (your feelings, fears, and desires). This is the part that communicates about *you* and gives the listener (your spouse) a window into your heart.

You may have noticed that we've included wants, desires, and longings in Heart Talk. These are important and powerful feelings, and in a truly great marriage, the desires of your heart will always be important to your spouse, as theirs will be to you. Sharing desires doesn't necessarily mean you'll get what you want. However, desires are a meaningful component of who you are, and having space to share your dreams and desires is simply a way of allowing yourself to be known. Hopefully, your spouse will be interested in not only knowing your desires but also sharing their desires and longings with you. Remember, however, that Heart Talk is about understanding each other and caring; it's not about problem-solving. It's a time for you and your spouse to connect heart to heart and clear up misunderstandings.

Here's another speaker tip: When you need to mention your spouse to give context to your feelings, make sure you keep the focus on yourself and your own yard. In other words, you can share what you perceive by observation and/or interpretation without shifting the focus to your spouse.

Because Vince doesn't share a lot about his feelings, I (Tara) often find myself trying to guess what might be going on over there. While I think I know him pretty well, I might begin the conversation this way: "When you acted x way, I assumed you felt x, though I genuinely don't know if that is the case. As a result of my interpretation, I ended up feeling x, y, and z." He might or might not respond to that observation. I simply share my feelings and what I imagine might be going on for him. If he is available to talk, I could say, "I would love to know what was actually going on for you when that happened." He would then be free to share—or not.

Finally, it's always a good idea to speak slowly, softly, and in small bites when you're the speaker. We have noticed that when people get excited, they tend to raise their voices, speak faster, and say too much all at once. If you want to keep the environment feeling safe, it can help to slow down and speak in a more subdued tone. Your spouse, as the listener, will need to reflect back what you've said to demonstrate their understanding. When you share your message a little at a time, it helps your spouse keep track and increases the likelihood that they will hear the important parts of your message. Usually it works best if you share just a few sentences at a time with the corresponding feelings. This sets up your spouse for success as a listener.

The following diagram shows the basic speaker-listener setup, including the three Heart Talk steps in the middle and the speaker's responsibilities on the left:

Slow, Soft, Small Bites

Speaker		Listener
Identify my feelings/emotions.	Identify	
Care about my heart/feelings. Ask for time.	Care	
Seek to be **understood** via an emotional message: "When ____ happens, I feel ____."	Understand	

The Listener Role

As a listener, you need to recognize that when your spouse is opening up and sharing their heart, they're inviting you into a sacred and intimate place. They are making themselves vulnerable and offering an opportunity for a deeper connection. Enjoying the fruits of this intimate connection requires the utmost care and caution, because carelessness in this space makes forging intimate bonds increasingly difficult going forward.

Listening in a heart talk is somewhat different from the type of listening you do in other kinds of communication. In this case, you are intentionally focused on hearing your spouse's heart and understanding their feelings. All other aspects of the communication are secondary. Using these listening skills at other times can be beneficial as well—they communicate safety and attentiveness, regardless of the topic—but in a heart talk, these skills are essential.

The listener uses the same three ICU steps as the speaker: Identify, Care, and Understand. The small difference is that the listener is focused on the speaker's heart, not their own. As a listener, you also want to make sure that you're cared up enough to be open and curious about what your spouse wants to share. These moments of communication can be a powerful influence as you and your spouse seek to build an intimate bond, so it's wise to prayerfully ask God to help you carefully handle your spouse's heart.

If you're not in a good place emotionally, or the timing isn't right, you may not be as careful with your spouse's heart as you need to be for a heart talk to remain safe. So when your spouse asks if you are available, be honest with yourself *and* your spouse. If you need time to do a care cycle or settle yourself, let them know. Suggest an alternative time and then be intentional about attending to yourself so that you can reconnect as quickly as possible. Remember that unnecessarily avoiding or delaying these conversations will likely send the message, "I don't care how you feel about that," which also tends to communicate, "And I don't care that much about you either!"

Once you're ready to listen and your spouse starts to share, the first step is to consciously listen for *feeling words*. You want to *identify* the heart message. What is this really about for your spouse? What is at the heart of it? What are they feeling? At this point, you aren't saying anything. You are simply tuning your ears to listen for the heart message and the feelings. You will hear the context as well, but listen carefully for the key details (the underlying message and emotions). It's possible your spouse won't plainly state their thoughts using feeling words, so you may need to read a little between the lines to identify specific emotions.

Imagine you're an art enthusiast, and you have come across a new piece of art by a famous artist. Naturally, the piece is framed in such a way as to show off the artistry captured in the scene. While you may notice the frame, it is only a supporting detail that helps you focus on the artist's work. The frame is not the art. When you're the listener in a heart talk, the message is the art. The topic related to the feelings is the frame. It supports the feelings and puts them in context, but it is not the focal point. You can notice the frame around the feelings, but your focus is on the feelings themselves.

The second step as a listener is to *care*. This is where you intentionally listen with your heart and not just with your head. As you hear the feelings, you attempt to understand their significance to your spouse. This is the essence of empathy—trying to see the world through someone else's eyes for a moment and sense what it would be like to be them. Again, you aren't saying anything yet. You are simply allowing what your spouse has shared to touch your heart. Since you love them, their feelings matter to you. You want to understand, and you want what is best for them. This is why it is so important for the listener to be cared up. You want to bring your best self to the enterprise of learning how to love your spouse well.

Even if you don't agree with the context (the frame), you want to focus on how their perception of what happened feels to them and impacts them. Having an attitude of curiosity is most helpful here.

We fully understand that focusing on your spouse's feelings can be challenging when they're sharing something in a context you disagree with, see differently, or feel differently about. But this is not the time to establish the "facts" or correct details of their story. Your goal as a listener is to hear their heart, period! We've counseled so many people who get stuck here. They passionately try to correct the details, thinking this will help the speaker feel different, feel better, or get the facts straight. Sometimes we have a hard time convincing them to let it go and just stay focused on the emotions.

This dilemma illustrates the old adage "People don't care what you know until they know that you care." It communicates real care if your spouse knows that you're seeking to understand their feelings, regardless of what may have generated them. In rare circumstances where correcting the facts is worthwhile, that can be done later.

When Jenni would share her feelings by saying, "When you said x, I felt x," my (Bob's) first thought was *But I never said that!* In reality, regardless of whether I said those exact words, that's what she remembered. I didn't have to agree with her memory of the conversation to hear her heart. In time I learned to resist the urge to correct facts.

Even when I'm reflecting back Jenni's heart message, I don't have to begin by saying, "Even though I never said that . . ." Instead, I can say, "When you heard me say x, you felt x." It's true that I may be thinking, *Even though I never said that*, but my focus is on her heart, *not* correcting the facts.

The final Heart Talk step in your role as a listener is to convey that you *understand* your spouse's message. Though it's now your turn to speak, you are *not* stepping into the role of a speaker because the focus is still on your spouse's feelings. Your sole purpose is to reflect back their emotional message. This is also not simply rote reflective listening. You want to convey to your spouse that you understand *and* care.

Initially, you may do this in a somewhat scripted way, but as you gain skill as a listener, it will become more natural. Reflecting back your spouse's heart message might sound something like this: "I hear you saying that when x happened, you felt x." You can repeat the exact words they used or the essence of their heart message, but always state it tentatively. You never want to *tell* a speaker how they feel. You are simply reflecting what you think you heard. They remain the authority on their feelings. By being tentative, you communicate respect.

Be careful to remain open and curious about what your spouse is sharing and what you are learning about them. Again, remember they are offering you a window into their soul, an opportunity to connect heart to heart.

After you reflect back what you think you heard, ask your spouse, "Did I get that right?" If your reflection wasn't accurate, ask if they can share their feelings again or correct whatever you missed. Always let your spouse be the expert on themselves. Listen with fresh ears, looking for what you may have missed. When your spouse says, "Yes, you got it," you can then ask, "Is there more?" If there is, you continue this process until they've finished and they feel understood and cared for. A heart talk is complete when the speaker feels understood, *not* when the listener thinks they understand!

A reminder to speakers here: Be careful not to overwhelm your spouse by trying to share everything at once. Pay attention to when either of you becomes saturated and needs a break. Some people have far more emotional capacity than others, so you may need to start small and work up to longer heart talks over time. Try to make these experiences feel safe, meaningful, and successful for both of you. Sometimes they won't be fun, but the relational confidence that grows from being able to effectively deal with sensitive or challenging topics will usually make the effort feel worthwhile.

When your spouse indicates they've shared all they wish to, and they feel heard, understood, and cared for, you can simply thank them for sharing and offer a heartfelt word of encouragement. At that point, you can either switch roles so that both of you have a chance to be heard or pause for now and switch when both of you are ready.

The following Heart Talk diagram now includes the listener's responsibilities on the right side:

Slow, Soft, Small Bites

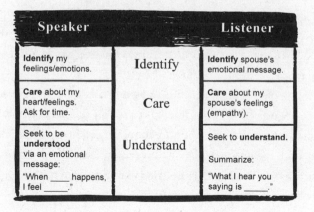

Speaker		Listener
Identify my feelings/emotions.	Identify	**Identify** spouse's emotional message.
Care about my heart/feelings. Ask for time.	Care	**Care** about my spouse's feelings (empathy).
Seek to be **understood** via an emotional message: "When _____ happens, I feel _____."	Understand	Seek to **understand.** Summarize: "What I hear you saying is _____."

When a heart talk is done well, you and your spouse will notice a sense of connection and a deeper understanding of each other. This can be true even after years of being together—the adventure of getting to know each other doesn't have to end. After more than forty years of marriage, Jenni and I (Bob) recently had a couple of heart talks that helped Jenni understand some things about me and the way I see things. She was startled and amazed! In fact, at first she looked at me with a puzzled expression and asked, "Do other people think like that?" I then shared that I actually knew a number of them. It turns out she'd never imagined it was possible to think or feel that way, or that others might have similar thoughts and feelings. We were both surprised that we'd never realized this misunderstanding existed. She was excited about this new revelation, and we both felt closer to each other as a result of our conversation. We were also encouraged about how this understanding would benefit us going forward.

We hope you're beginning to see how all the tools we've been talking about work together to create an environment where deep connection and empowered love can grow in your marriage. But we haven't yet addressed the most commonly asked relational question: "So what do we *do*?" In other words: "How do we effectively manage our differences, come up with strategies for doing life together that we can both feel good about, and truly resolve conflict?"

Well, you've made it this far, and we finally have everything we need to answer those questions and set you up to be wildly successful. Next, we'll offer one more tool that can help you tackle the big issues of life and marriage in a way that feels like you and your spouse are functioning as close friends and teammates.

10

WINNING
AS A TEAM

SATAN, THE MORTAL ENEMY OF EVERY spouse, marriage, and family, wants us all dead and our families destroyed. He skillfully uses deceptive tactics to drive wedges between us. His basic battle strategy is to divide and conquer, and he regularly uses power struggles to achieve his despicable objectives. When you get into a conflict with your spouse, who do you normally see as the enemy? Your spouse! In that moment—when you see your spouse as your enemy—Satan wins. Chalk one up for your adversary: bad guys 1; good guys 0.

When two spouses square off as adversaries, the outcome is already decided. Why? Because, by God's design, marriage is a team sport, and when you are on the same team, there are only two possible outcomes. You both win or you both lose. There is no such thing as a win-lose outcome in marriage—ever! This is a lie from the pit of hell. It doesn't exist. It *can't* exist. As teammates, you win together or you lose together. Jesus made this perfectly clear in Matthew 12:25 (and in other accounts) when He said, "Every kingdom divided against itself is laid waste, and no city or house divided against itself will stand."

How do you make sure the good guys win? How do you make sure *you* win? How do you make your family strong and your marriage a delightful refuge to run *to*, not *from*? The key is to fully embrace the reality that you and your spouse are teammates, and then do everything possible to make sure your team always wins! Do you think that sounds unrealistic—like a nice fairy tale? Well, it's not, because we serve a God who is 100 percent devoted to unity. He is the creator of the universe! He is also the ruler of the universe, and He will ultimately bring everything into unity with Him. And given the opportunity, He will faithfully bring a husband and wife into unity with each other.

We aren't talking here about simply finding solutions you can put up with or tolerate. We're talking about complete and total win-win solutions. Just to be clear, we define a win-win solution as nothing short of an outcome you *both* feel great about. We've often heard that when you bump into your differences in marriage and are at odds with each other, the key is to find a good compromise. Each of you gives a little, and then you can brainstorm options both of you can live with. Yuck! That sounds a lot like accepting mediocrity. And who gets excited about their marriage slowly trending toward mediocre? Not us!

Most people who marry are fundamentally different from each other. Jenni and I (Bob) are radically different in many ways. And as you might expect, our wonderfully unique characteristics and preferences frequently put us at odds with each other. Yet we continue allowing our Lord to faithfully bring us into unity with each other and with Him. This is also true for the large number of colleagues we work with who apply the principles in this book to their marriages—and it is true for many of the thousands of couples we've served. Our Lord is in charge. He is faithful and available. We need to accept this and allow Him to have His way with our marriages.

A marriage that blesses God and serves His purposes is not embroiled in conflict. That's the enemy's game. Instead, the Lord wants you to deal openly and respectfully with the challenges your differences reveal. His plan is for you and your spouse to work through these challenges as friends, lovers, and teammates, *not* as adversaries. When you fight, it's only against your common enemies, *not* each other. You have each other's backs. Your battles are against the forces of evil, and you fight them side by side.

How do you do that? How can you deal well with your many differences and end up with no-compromise win-win solutions?

The Steps to a Win-Win

Let's get practical. You are now operating as teammates and partners on this journey, ready every day to face the challenges this life assures you. You need tangible tools that work in real time when you're facing difficult obstacles. There are, of course, many techniques to help couples resolve conflict. If you've found something that works well, keep using it. But we want to offer a simple tool we've developed called *Work Talk* that is straightforward and relatively foolproof. We think you'll find this tool helpful for two reasons. First, it's a feedback loop. When you encounter conflicts in your marriage, you'll use the information you've gained along the journey to adjust your strategies and work toward a resolution until your team wins. If at first you don't succeed, try, try again.

Second, this tool is based on God's desire and intent to bring you into unity with each other and with Him, without compromise. Your goal now is to find options you both feel great about—and accept nothing less.

This process will likely test your faith, but it will also provide opportunities to experience firsthand how real and available God is. You will need to surrender to Him and His care to witness this unity. So if you're ready to proceed, we'll lay out our seven-step process.

Step 1: Adopt and Apply a No-Losers Policy

The first step to finding a win-win solution when you encounter conflicts in your marriage is to adopt a no-losers policy. Remember that God created marriage as a team sport—both of you win or both of you lose. Accept this as a fact. It's God's design, and you can't change it. Since He is the Creator, He decides how things work. Like the laws of physics or nature, which He also created, you can't change this basic law of relationships. God's law prevails. However, when you learn to appreciate and work within the parameters of this law, you'll set your marriage up to win by surrendering to God's sovereignty over your decisions.

Next, you need to apply this no-losers policy the moment you find yourself in conflict with your teammate. In my (Tara's) marriage, it might sound something like this: "Vince, we're obviously not seeing eye to eye on this, but we know we're teammates, and God wants us in unity. Before we do anything to work this out, I want you to know up front that I won't accept any solution unless we *both* like it. I want our team to win. I'm ready to see God help us overcome this and take us there. Are you with me?"

Once both of you establish this basic commitment, you're ready to function as a team. As followers of Christ, you're perfectly positioned to watch Him bring you and your spouse into unity. Sometimes even miraculously.

Step 2: Heart-Talk the Issue

In the previous chapter, we laid out our Heart Talk tool and mentioned that it wasn't designed for problem-solving. In its purest form, this is absolutely true. Don't use Heart Talk as the *primary* tool for overcoming your differences. However, as part of a win-win strategy, it has significant practical value. Since you're striving toward a solution you both feel great about, taking a few minutes to hear each other's hearts on the matter at hand is, in essence, mining critical data. Without first knowing how each of you feels about the issue, including what concerns you, what you like and don't like, what you want and don't want, and why, the likelihood of finding a solution you both feel great about would be like shooting in the dark and hoping you hit something. Why subject yourselves to that level of frustration and futility? Do everything you can to get clear about the thoughts and feelings involved so you know what you're working with. Then lay it all on the table so it's in full view as you proceed.

Don't judge or challenge each other's thoughts, preferences, or feelings. Comments like "You want what?" or "Why would you want that?" or "That doesn't even make sense!" are judgmental statements. Make this a safe space too. You are different, and that's only a problem if you make it one. God is more than able to take the differences He created and use them to bless each of you, your team, and His Kingdom.

Step 3: Pray Together for Unity

With all your differences in full view, pray together for God's help finding a solution you both can feel great about. Know that this is His desire and intent, and He is more than able and willing to take you there. This process may challenge your faith, but it will help you see the degree to which you believe that God can work in the middle of your conflict—maybe even intervening in a miraculous way that enables you to overcome a big point of contention. Praying together will also reveal the extent to which you are willing to surrender control to the Lord. Both of these challenges are your focus. At least you will know what you're working with and in what ways you need to ask for God's help.

One of the most exciting aspects of prayer is that you're doing it *together*. The moment you join together and ask God to bring you to a solution, you'll both feel great and have instantly restored unity! You are now working as a team to find solutions, strategies, and opportunities. While you haven't solved any problems yet, the journey toward a win-win solution feels remarkably better from here. You have locked arms as teammates and are committed to working together.

Step 4: Brainstorm Options

This is the key Work Talk step where you lay out ideas for solving whatever you're struggling with in your marriage. Try not to overthink this at first. Just spend some time together brainstorming ideas and jotting them down so you can evaluate them later. This helps get the creative juices flowing. Don't be too concerned about whether you'll both like the ideas. Focus on getting stuff down on paper.

When you run out of straightforward and reasonable possibilities, try thinking outside the box. We call this a *green-light thinking session*. It's easy to get locked into such a narrow focus that you can miss more creative options, perhaps even a divinely inspired surprise. So be willing to stretch your minds a little and explore seemingly fringe ideas.

In addition to green-light thinking sessions, look for other kinds of Work Talk opportunities. For instance, if you know someone who has special knowledge or experience with the issue you're working through, consulting with that person might yield gold. Or a trusted source on the internet might have the perfect solution. When brainstorming, try a variety of methods you both feel good about.

Step 5: Evaluate Your Options and Pick One . . . or Wait

Once your brainstorming session is done, or you've exhausted a previously agreed-upon time limit, evaluate the pros and cons of each idea. Pay close attention to how each of you feels about the options you're considering. Remember, you are searching for solutions you both *feel* great about, so your feelings matter. Tune in to the Lord, too, asking Him to guide you toward a win-win solution.

The goal is to find a win-win, not to convince your spouse of the merits of your favored options. If your spouse says, "That option doesn't feel like a win to me," it's a loss for the team. While it may be helpful to ask why your spouse feels it's a loss (so you can better evaluate other options), you still need to cross it off your list. That goes for any option that feels like a loss to either of you for any reason. If you're unable to find an option you both feel great about, you may want to return to this step later. You may even want to heart-talk the issue to understand each other on a deeper level while looking for new possibilities.

As you review your list, put a check mark next to the options that feel like a win to both of you, cross off any that feel like a loss to either of you, and put a question mark next to any that require more discussion. As you get closer to deciding next steps, make sure you both feel good about trying something that may not work. Sometimes the best way to find effective options is through trial and error.

Eventually, most couples find solutions that work best for them. It really doesn't matter whether anyone else likes how you solve your problems, as long as you both feel great about the solution, without compromise, and it lines up with Scripture.

More than once, I (Bob) ended up liking a solution that Jenni originally suggested but I really disliked at first. Somewhere along the line, God changed my heart, or I heard something from Jenni that made me see the solution differently. At other times, Jenni had a change of heart about an option she didn't like at first. There were also some quirky situations in which we found creative solutions that neither of us initially considered or we constructed win-wins by combining elements of both our ideas.

If you can't find a solution you both like, it's often best to wait and try again later. We have found that when both spouses are genuinely seeking God but can't reach unity, one of two things is happening: Either the Lord is using their disunity to protect them from making a decision they'll regret, or He wants them to pause because a better solution is coming. Obviously, God sees far more than our limited minds can perceive, and if we act prematurely, we can miss His best. Disunity over a solution should grab your attention. It may be a vital sign to pause and listen for God's direction.

If you feel stuck, conduct a personal gut check. As fallen creatures, we can easily fool ourselves into thinking we are seeking God's best when we're really trying to get our spouses and God to agree with our ideas. Ask yourself, *Am I really committed to a no-losers policy and trusting God and the process to get us there, or am I unconsciously holding out, hoping that God will shift my spouse's heart toward what I want?* If an honest gut check indicates that you're holding out, don't judge yourself. Most people struggle with this. Simply take some time to explore your feelings using the Care

Cycle. Looking inward can reveal what is making it hard for you to release control and let God direct the process.

Once you've attended to whatever your gut check revealed, see if you're ready to recommit to the no-losers policy. Then make a fresh run through the seven steps. When you find yourself needing to wait for unity, don't miss the opportunity to have a heart talk with your spouse and share what waiting feels like for each of you. This can be a wonderful way to reconnect and remind yourselves that you're still in this together.

Step 6: Try Out Your Solution

After you've landed on a solution you both feel great about, give it a try. A trial run will help you and your spouse determine whether it actually works. It may be an awesome solution, it may be so-so, or it may be terrible, but you'll never know unless you try it out. If it ends up being a mediocre or terrible solution, don't let that discourage you. Learn from the experience and use the information you gathered in the process to enhance your search for other options.

Step 7: Evaluate Your Success and Rework
Your Plan as Needed

At some predetermined time, check in with each other and ask how the solution is working. If both of you give it a rousing thumbs-up, you're there. Just keep doing what you've agreed to. However, if either of you is less than happy with the solution, cycle back through the seven steps. Recommit to the no-losers policy. Heart-talk what worked and what didn't. Continue asking God for guidance. Brainstorm ways to tweak your plan based on what you've learned so far. Find a new win-win solution and give it a try. Then evaluate how it worked for each of you. Keep going until you arrive at a solution you both love.

✝

Here's a brief recap of the seven steps to a win-win solution:

1. Adopt and apply a no-losers policy.
2. Heart-talk the issue.
3. Pray together for unity.
4. Brainstorm options.
5. Evaluate your options and pick one . . . or wait.
6. Try out your solution.
7. Evaluate your success and rework your plan as needed.

Allow me (Bob) to share a real-life example that illustrates how this win-win process has worked in our marriage. Over the past couple of years, Jenni and I faced a series of life-altering decisions. Prior to the COVID-19 pandemic, we decided to finish some home-improvement projects that were needed to get our house in top shape. We downsized to this house after our kids launched into adulthood, and we absolutely loved it. It served us well for thirteen years, and we knew the improvements would make it even better.

But then God began to move in each of us in unexpected ways. Once the pandemic lockdowns hit and we had more time for projects, Jenni sensed that God was calling us to "simplify and become mobile." At first these words made no sense to either of us, but we had felt His divine stirring before, so we prayerfully asked for clarity and guidance. All we heard back was the same message: "Simplify and become mobile." We were still confused, since we weren't looking to go anywhere.

However, as empty nesters, we realized that we'd accumulated quite a bit of stuff. As we looked ahead to our senior years, simplifying did make good sense, so Jenni took on the painstaking task of going through our belongings and paring them down. After finishing this task and some remaining home-improvement projects, Jenni and I were elated with the results. The house was in the most beautiful condition ever, and we were actually able to park both cars in the garage at the same time! (Simplifying also meant letting the kids know that Mom and Dad's house would no longer be a free storage unit.)

We were enjoying life in our house even more than before. Then God began to move in each of our hearts in a strange way. Home interest rates had dropped to historic lows, and the housing market went nuts! Prices skyrocketed, and houses were selling so fast, the available inventory plummeted. Our house value began to move to levels we never dreamed possible. We wondered if God was nudging us to sell, but then we'd ask, "And *then* what?"

A side note here: Several years earlier, Jenni and I sensed God calling us to become debt-free so we'd be available to respond to whatever He might have for us. We had made progress but had never quite pulled it off. We could see how this call to eliminate our debt was connected to the Lord's current leading to simplify and become mobile. Through prayer, each of us understood that God was leading us to trust Him and put the house on the market.

As is often the case with trusting God, He didn't reveal what would be next, but we both heard Him and began taking the steps. We were unified in this decision, but we also knew it would lead to a big move and an uncertain future. We realized we needed to apply the win-win principles we'd been learning over the years, so we established a clear no-losers policy, agreeing that we would move forward only when we were in complete unity.

Our game plan was to put our belongings in storage and, after the house sold, temporarily move into the investment property we owned in Branson, Missouri. We'd lose a little money on rent, but the condo would give us a place to live while we tried to find a new house in a crazy seller's market.

So the house was listed, and within a few days, we accepted a full-price offer. With only thirty days to move out, we rented a big storage unit so we could transfer the contents of our smaller unit over to the bigger one. But when we entered the smaller unit, we were horrified to find cockroaches all over our belongings. Everything was ruined. We instantly understood that we needed a plan B, but we didn't have one. After our initial shock, a little hyperventilating, and some understandable tears, we prayed for guidance, asking God to open our minds to His plan and bring us into unity with each other and with Him. Then Jenni and I *heart-talked the issue*, sharing many unexpected feelings with each other.

Next, we *brainstormed options*. One possibility we hadn't considered was to rent temporarily. We hadn't rented a house in many years, and frankly, most of what we saw on the rental market was either way too expensive or not a place we'd want to visit, let alone live in. But the Lord encouraged us to keep looking, and so we did, *evaluating our options* along the way. We ended up finding a nice little house that was reasonably priced. The landlord was great, even agreeing to a six-month lease that would work with our plans to buy a home as soon as possible. It seemed like the perfect solution, so we decided to *try it out*.

Now debt-free, we moved into our tiny rental home and began an incredibly time-consuming search for a new house in one of the strongest seller's markets in history. Houses would come on the market and sell within hours. We had a skilled real-estate agent, but there was only so much he could do. So Jenni and I spent every spare hour scouring online listings. We also had a heart talk about the things each of us really wanted in our next house. Some of our wants were similar, but others were very different. Yet we reaffirmed that unless we were both in complete unity, we wouldn't buy, no matter what. That required a lot of trust in God's direction, as well as patience throughout the process. We looked at dozens of houses over many weeks, but we could never get on the same page. One time, we were just about to sign on a house when a previously undisclosed detail was revealed that made it an absolute no-go for Jenni. I was slightly frustrated, because I really liked that house, but I trusted God and Jenni, and we awkwardly got up and walked away. *Okay, God, what was that about?* I wondered.

A few weeks later, a house popped up on the market that looked promising. I immediately called our agent, but with so many interested buyers, we weren't able to get a showing until late that evening. By the time we arrived, it was pitch-black outside, and there were already two offers on the house. It desperately needed updating, but with a little work, it was just what we had been looking for. It was also thousands of dollars less expensive than the one we'd almost purchased. Jenni and I were in complete unity and felt that God wanted us to buy this house. So late that night, we submitted a fairly creative offer.

The next morning, Jenni couldn't remember what the house looked like and asked if we could see it in the daylight. So we drove by the property and agreed that we still felt good about it. Later that morning, our agent informed us that there were multiple offers on the house, including one cash offer that matched ours. We thought we were sunk! But then we learned that the sellers had requested an earnest money payment of $1,000 from the cash buyers, who promptly said no. The sellers were so put off, they rejected that offer and came to us. We immediately agreed to the earnest request, and the sellers so appreciated the way our agent handled it all that they knocked $2,500 off the price of the house. *Who does that?*

Today we absolutely love our house and the freedom that comes from being debt free. We also love the way we handled every step of the journey—and the way God's loving hand guided us through the process, even when we struggled to be patient. We trusted God and each other and the win-win process for a *successful outcome*.

Our "simplify and become mobile" calling led to some big decisions with many layers of complexity that took months to work out using the seven steps to a win-win solution. We use these same steps in any situation where strong feelings are involved and unity is difficult to find. Most of the time when Jenni and I are faced with a decision, big or small, we cruise through our differences in a flash. We're determined to pursue unity with each other and our Lord, no matter what. This win-win strategy works because God always brings stubborn and strong-willed people like us into agreement anytime we surrender our hearts to Him and trust His plan.

Now that fear has virtually disappeared when we face conflicts and challenges in our marriage, we find that unity comes much more quickly. Before we adopted the no-losers policy, we often feared that at least one of us would have to settle for a solution we didn't really like. But now we have total confidence that if either of us doesn't like an option, the other will immediately respond, "Then it won't work for me either." Jenni and I are a team, and either we both feel great about a solution or we keep looking.

Eliminating fear in managing your conflicts is one of the best ways we know to change the relational scoreboard so that it reads, "Good Guys: 1; Bad Guys: 0"!

Setting Healthy and Righteous Boundaries

Earlier in the book, we discussed the importance of establishing and maintaining healthy boundaries in our marriages. As we've said before, many (or maybe most) problems in marriage can be traced back to misplaced responsibilities—either taking responsibility for things that aren't ours to take or not taking responsibility for things that are. Using the Healthy Marriage Model, we discussed boundaries in a healthy marriage (remember the circles?) and various applications of those boundaries, along with their corresponding responsibilities. Here, we'll map out an effective step-by-step process for setting healthy boundaries as a couple.

The fundamental role of a boundary is clarifying what belongs inside your circle of responsibility and what does not. In relationships, where does your responsibility stop, and where does everything else begin? What is yours and what is not? Remember, clearly knowing what belongs where, whose responsibility it is, and whose it isn't has a direct impact on your personal peace and power.

But we all make mistakes. When personal lines are crossed and our well-being is at stake, in an effort to care for ourselves, we may attempt to get another person to stop or start doing something. The problem with this approach is that we tend to define success in taking care of ourselves as getting another free-will agent (like our spouses) to act in a way we want or need them to. This approach puts *you* in a disempowered position, because there is no righteous way to control another person's behavior. Any effort to get your spouse to do whatever you want or need, even subtly, forces you to become controlling or manipulative, which is never consistent with who God created you to be.

Since you're still responsible to take care of yourself, what can you do instead? You need to establish and maintain healthy, righteous boundaries. Recognize that the most basic aspect of caring for yourself is to make sure your heart is open and connected to God, your source. The key to establishing any righteous boundary is taking full responsibility for ensuring that your heart stays open and connected, rather than seeking to control another person or their behavior.

Let's set up the steps with a simple example. Say Vince did something that really set me (Tara) off, and I started to yell at him. Clearly, I'm not cared up in this scenario. And while Vince's actions may have genuinely hurt my feelings, my yelling causes him to close his heart and disconnect not just from me but from God as well. This isn't good for either of us. We both need Vince's heart connected to God. What can he righteously do? Well, he first needs to accept that the doors to his heart are his responsibility, not mine. He also needs to recognize that I have a God-given right to yell, though it may not be a righteous response. And I have the right to exercise my will this way, though I certainly don't have the power to make Vince do what I want him to.

Vince alone is responsible for taking good care of himself, which I sincerely hope he'll do when I show up so compromised. Since shutting the door of his heart to God will never accomplish that, he needs to open his heart and get cared up so we can resolve our conflict.

Now let's explore the key steps Vince can take to establish a healthy and righteous boundary in this scenario.

Step 1: Make a Request

The first step in setting a righteous boundary is to make a request to calmly and respectfully talk about the problem. Vince needs to actively create a space that will enable his heart and spirit to reopen, without trying to control my behavior. It might sound something like this: "Tara, I know you're upset, and that matters, but I'm shutting down in the face of your yelling. Is there any possibility we could talk about this without the attack?"

Now, for this to be a request, it *must* be acceptable for me to say no. Otherwise, it's a demand, not a genuine request. All demands are controlling, never righteous. No matter how ridiculously sweet the request sounds, if I say no—or I keep yelling (which is also saying no)—and Vince gets upset, then his request was more like a demand.

If I say no to his request, Vince is still responsible for keeping his heart open and connected to God. But what can he do when his request isn't honored? That brings us to the next step.

Step 2: Have a Contingency Plan

A genuine request always allows for the possibility that the other person might decline. If I decline Vince's request, he must either try again or try something else. In this scenario, he might decide to step back or walk away. But his *reason* for doing so reveals whether he is acting in a righteous and healthy way or is shutting down and avoiding further conflict. If he walks away to teach me a lesson or point out how wrong I am for yelling, there is nothing righteous in that approach—even if he is right! It's just a controlling and manipulative response. If he is shutting down to avoid his feelings, that only dishonors him. The reason for stepping back must always be to create space for his heart to stay open and connected to God.

In our situation, as Vince steps back from engaging, he needs to ask God right away to help him reopen his heart. Feeling compassion for himself will typically be the first sign he's getting there. That doesn't mean feeling *sorry* for himself, like thinking, *I hate this! Why does she always have to be like that?* Compassion is more like thinking, *Ouch, that feels terrible. My heart is shutting down, and I'm cut off from God. I don't want to stay here. Lord, please help me reopen and reconnect. I don't like this version of me.*

Feeling compassion for me is another sign that Vince is opening up. He might be thinking, *Lord, Tara must be feeling terrible too. She gets like this only when she is really hurting or scared. Be with her, Lord. She needs You too.* Vince can feel compassion for me because he is no longer in the line of fire. He has physically and emotionally stepped back and has taken solid steps to care for himself. His heart is opening back up, and he is again being the strong, loving man God created him to be. He can soon bring that version of Vince back to me. And in all this, he is loving me, caring well for himself, and honoring God.

This turnaround is not just hard to imagine; it's also difficult to pull off in the middle of a conflict. But it really works! Through intentional focus and practice, you can successfully establish healthy and righteous boundaries for everyone's benefit.

Over the years, Jenni has demonstrated this principle in many ways in our marriage. I (Bob) am often tempted to think she's being self-centered and unrighteous when she steps back from engaging with me. But she has continually helped me see the difference between righteous and selfish actions. Remember when Jenni climbed out of our bedroom window to escape my self-righteous rant? Well, I need to tell you the rest of the story. When she finally returned, I told her I was upset that she bailed on us and God. I believed that driving away was an attempt to control me and our marriage rather than staying and trying to work things out.

She paused and gave me a curious look. Then she said, "Bob, why are you making this about you? I wasn't trying to control you. Do what you want to do. I was just taking care of me! I felt unsafe and unloved, and my heart was closing up. I needed to get away so God could lead me to a better place. And now I'm back with my heart reopened. And just so you know, that's what I will do from now on when any interaction with you doesn't feel good, and I start going to a bad place inside. It has to be good for either of us to stay put."

Jenni has been true to her word. I couldn't see it at first because it felt as if she was making the conflict about me and was just trying to control me. But her consistency in establishing boundaries over the years has, with God's help, enabled me to see how right she was. The goal of a healthy and righteous Christ-centered boundary is always to take good care of yourself so that you can continue to be the person God created you to be, bringing your best self to all your most important relationships and to the world. That is what honors God most!

Learning to Wait Well

Closely related to boundaries is the idea of waiting well. When your spouse establishes a boundary, it can often feel like a wall. None of us likes to be faced with a wall because it feels as if we're being shut out. And in a way, we are. For a time, I (Bob) felt as if Jenni had erected an impenetrable wall, but she needed that wall to reestablish her safety and care for herself, which is always best for her and our marriage. While not everyone does good self-care behind their walls the way Jenni did, the reason why people erect them is the same: They don't feel safe.

What can you do when you're faced with a wall in your relationship? Some unhealthy responses might be trying to tear it down or climb over it, which is what I typically did. Or you could walk away and give up on the person behind the wall because staying is too painful. But neither of these approaches makes the one who is waiting feel better or the one behind the wall feel safe.

A healthy, God-honoring response when you encounter a wall

is to seek God's guidance on learning to wait well. Waiting is a form of loving your spouse that is based on honor and respect. Each of us has the power to choose to be open and available or closed and unavailable. God won't force you to open up, even when it might be in your best interest to do so. Likewise, you have the opportunity to honor and respect your spouse's right to choose not to engage with you, even when it's disappointing.

You won't always know what caused your spouse to erect a wall. But the most loving, respectful, and safest thing you can do is recognize that something has upset your spouse and caused them to feel unsafe. In response, they closed their heart and shut down. You can let them know you're sad and miss them, but any attempt to disregard their choice will feel disrespectful and uncaring to them.

You can also attend to what you're directly responsible for: yourself. Care for your heart by focusing on any fears and hurts you feel as a result of your spouse's decision to be closed and unavailable. Ask the Lord to be with you and fill you. Strive to be the best possible version of yourself and continue to make valuable use of your time as the Lord directs. This can help put you in the ideal posture to reconnect with your spouse if, or when, they are ready to reengage. When they do, they'll find you cared up, filled up, open, and available to help move the relationship to a better place for both of you.

People regularly ask us, "How long should I wait?" To their chagrin, our answer is always "As long as it takes." It could be hours, days, weeks, or longer. It is not your job to pressure your spouse to do the work they need to do behind their wall. It is your job to keep the door to your heart open to your source (God) and remain cared up as you wait. That's waiting well! God loves your spouse more than you do, and any work they need to do is completely between them and the Lord. It is all in your spouse's yard, and thus, it's completely their responsibility. However, as you wait, God can fill you, grow you, love you, and give you whatever you need to stay open and well attended to, even if it takes years. Obviously, this is not preferred or desirable. But it *is* respectful and loving.

In some ways, this is how I (Tara) experience my marriage to Vince. Please understand, there are some wonderful things about our marriage, and it's getting better all the time. I am so thankful for Vince! At the same time, I'm still waiting in some areas of our relationship. I don't know if I will ever experience my deepest desires for the marriage of my dreams, but I'm grateful for what we have. All these tools Bob and I have been sharing with you really do work!

I (Bob) never thought in a million years that Jenni and I could get as far as we have. There were moments when our marriage looked hopeless! But miracles are always possible, by God's grace, when both spouses surrender to Him and use these tools. No guarantees, but we know of no better way to greatly increase the odds.

Your journey together is an amazing love story in the making, with plenty of twists and turns, unexpected moments, victories and setbacks, breakthroughs and challenges. God can also move powerfully in your relationship with *Him* as you wait. He will show you more ways to be everything He created you to be and to love your spouse just as they are today.

I (Tara) have never been more excited to see and love Vince for who he is (with the Lord's help). I don't know where, or how far, our love story goes from here, but I'm all in, fully committed to using what I've learned in my own yard to the best of my ability as Vince and I continue this journey together. I wouldn't trade what we have, or who Vince is, for anything. And I believe with all my heart that things will keep getting better for us as I continue to grow personally, and as God continues to work with and in my husband, His beloved son.

The same can be true for your marriage because of who our Lord is and how committed He is to you, His child. Now, that's empowering!

11

LEAVING
A LEGACY

THROUGHOUT THIS BOOK, we have made the case that the best starting place for a great marriage is to assume radical responsibility for your own emotional, spiritual, physical, and mental well-being (ESPM). As an imperfect person desiring to become more conformed to the image of Christ, you need to embrace personal responsibility to initiate this journey. You also need to recognize that God created and designed you to live in connection with Him. He deeply loves you and wants nothing more than for you to be whole, healthy, and fully empowered to find your purpose in His Kingdom. Your life has no greater value or significance than when you are operating in the middle of God's fabulous plan for you.

From there, you can join with a complementary person of the opposite sex to complete God's design for the family, which is the foundation of safe and satisfying relationships. The marriage relationship is the cornerstone of God's plan for creating and growing His family. He loves us and wants this union to bless, challenge, and grow those of us who are called to marry. Throughout the journey together as husband and wife, we embrace the adventure of loving, supporting, and encouraging each other as we face the many twists and turns that life on this planet guarantees.

As we all know, some moments in marriage are thrilling, some are agreeable, and some are pleasurable. Others are heartbreaking, terrifying, and difficult. You and your spouse are partners on this journey, and neither of you ever really knows what lies around the next bend. What you do know, however, is that as faithful friends, trusted lovers, and skillful teammates, you will face the challenges you encounter *together*.

But the story doesn't end there! We are here on this planet with a purpose that is bigger than our individual lives. In fact, our lives are meant to touch everyone around us and reflect God's love to a hurting world. You can offer hope to the hopeless and encouragement to the discouraged. You can help others see that their lives truly matter and that how they live can make a real difference in the world. God has created everyone on purpose for a purpose, whether or not they realize it!

When you live well as a follower of Christ, you leave a genuine legacy for those your life touches. This legacy can have an impact that endures for generations. Many of the parents we talk to want to leave a positive legacy for their children. They don't want their kids to grow up in broken homes like they did but to have a healthier model of marriage. Beyond that, they want their children to have *hope* for a better tomorrow and a profound *security* that their lives matter and that they can be a meaningful part of the solution.

Hope for a better tomorrow was a common theme that emerged in my (Tara's) research. All the couples I interviewed talked about missing out on a healthy model for marriage when they were growing up and wanting to do things differently for their kids. Anne said, "[Mitchell and I] were both very committed to doing everything possible to stop the negative generational impact of divorce in our families." They were also the most excited about sharing all they had learned not only with their adult children but also with friends, small groups at church, and anyone else they thought would benefit. They wanted their legacy to impact many more people than simply themselves.

I (Tara) was blessed with parents who modeled not only staying together when times got rough but also doing the work to make things better. They had many struggles when I was in my late teens and early twenties, but divorce was never an option for them. They refused to simply exist in an unhappy marriage. My father was the first one to make the shift. He turned to God and surrendered everything to Him, including his marriage. "No more doing it my way," he would say.

My father prayed for unity with my mother, and he trusted God to do whatever was needed. When he had a job opportunity that involved moving, he refused to do so without my mom's buy-in. He prayed, *God, You are a God of unity, so if You want us to move, You have to make it okay with Sheila, because I won't go without her buy-in.*

I love my father's boldness. God is big enough to handle that kind of prayer!

Soon after, my mom was willing to move without any pressure from him. And while they were living on the East Coast, she turned more fully to God and surrendered her life to Him. Both of my parents made their marriage a priority, and it slowly started turning around. They would say that marriage is hard at times, but what they gained from weathering that challenging period made their relationship so much richer than it was before. After fifty years of marriage, they love one another deeply and thoroughly enjoy each other's company.

Their marriage is an encouragement not only to their children but also to their nieces, nephews, grandkids, and the married couples they serve as Hope Restored hosts in Canada. My parents live in full view of a world that is watching to see if Christian marriages really can be different. Many couples seek what they have. My parents are creating a legacy, as God intended. That is His desire for all of us.

As you remain plugged into the Lord, striving to be who you were created to be and bringing all the gifts He has endowed you with to accomplish all He has put before you, you are truly empowered to love. You may not be able to *control* much of what occurs in this world, but you can have real *influence*. Sometimes that influence may involve helping make circumstances and relationships materially better. Other times, it may involve modeling how to manage difficulties and challenges while remaining connected to our Lord and manifesting His grace.

As we have learned over time, even when you think you're invisible—when it seems as if no one notices what you do—people around you are taking note of your life. They might not be the people you think are watching, or even people you *want* to be watching, but they notice how you live. We regularly hear stories from people who paid close attention to the way another person lived their life, even in the midst of difficult circumstances. These observers often recount how that person's example became the inspiration for how they choose to live their lives today, and who they want to be.

Missed Opportunities

Obviously, the opposite can be true too. Sometimes we live our lives in completely uninspiring ways that support only hopelessness and despair. Or we may miss opportunities to help those we love to see the full significance of who they are and how much potential influence they have.

As you focus on improving yourself and your marriage, you will also improve the legacy you leave. A legacy is usually far less about individual moments of success or failure than it is about the cumulative impact of a life well lived.

One of the times I (Bob) feel the most sadness is when I look back at significant missed opportunities while Jenni and I were raising our children. I have attempted to follow God and serve Him well since I accepted Jesus as my Savior the day before our wedding. Sometimes my faith is clear and strong; other times I've lost my focus. But I have always found my way back to my commitment and desire to faithfully fulfill the reason He brought me here.

As Jenni and I began having children, the Lord helped me see the importance of being the spiritual leader of my family. But I felt completely unprepared for that role. My wife, who led me to the Lord, was so much more spiritually mature than I was, and I felt terribly inadequate by comparison. Eventually I went back to school and received a degree in biblical studies. I was even a pastor for a short time. But I never seemed to consistently succeed in my job as spiritual leader of my family.

What I now know is that I had a largely mistaken understanding of what a spiritual leader's role and responsibilities actually are. I thought the main job was to lead family devotions and look for ways to help my kids learn more about our Lord, pointing out moments when we could see Him at work. As valuable as all that is, I wasn't very good at any of it—spiritual consistency with my family wasn't my strong suit. But that wasn't my worst failing. I have come to realize that I was a *colossal* failure at the single most important part of being a spiritual leader: allowing my children to watch me struggle, then turn to the Lord for help and grow in my faith as He met me in my mess.

Yes, my children watched some parts of my faith journey. I've now been in full-time ministry for many years, and every one of my kids would tell you that I am serious about my faith. They each respect me and hold me in high regard because they have watched me grow and become a much better man. They also witnessed the transformation of their parents' marriage from a strained and contentious relationship to a generally harmonious and loving one. Our eldest daughter even flies home for a week periodically so she can bask in "Mommy and Daddy really loving each other well," since for so many years it was hit or miss.

The problem is that each of my children believes that the reason I have grown and improved as a person, and why I have helped improve our marriage as well, is because I am basically a man of good character who finally found my way. But nothing could be further from the truth—and I wish they knew it!

The truth is, things have gotten better for Jenni and me because I have consistently allowed my patient and loving heavenly Father to have access to my life and my heart. He helps me see the areas where I'm stuck and missing the mark, and then He gently guides me. In spite of all my shortcomings, He provides strength and faith, guidance and direction. He has waited when I've turned my back on Him, or when I've simply insisted on doing things my way. And when I finally turn back to Him, He always meets me with open and loving arms. *Welcome back, My son*, He says. *Are you ready to go forward with Me again?*

My kids have seen the *results* of my growth, but I didn't allow them to watch the journey. I suppose I found my shortcomings too embarrassing and was afraid that I wouldn't follow through on my commitments to change for the better. I was too proud to let them see that I didn't have it all together. But the most authentic, raw, and real part of my faith journey was that slow process of humble growth. Modeling a genuine journey of faith—demonstrating what that walk looks like in the trenches—is spiritual leadership at its best!

Had I allowed my kids to witness my journey up close and personal, they would have seen the way God met me in my inadequacy and weakness and transformed me over time into a man far closer to the one He created me to be! It would have been as real for them as it was for me. I could have shown them the way and encouraged them to tap into those same life-giving resources. But I didn't—and they haven't—and there is nothing I grieve more in this life!

It's Not Too Late

Young people today are desperately searching for anything authentic, and they rail against anything that smacks of hypocrisy and lip service. When I (Bob) was a child, I would occasionally challenge my mother's directives because they seemed to contradict what she actually did. Her regular retort was "Do as I say, not as I do." That response always upset me, and I have made a point of never using it with my children—or anyone else for that matter. I want my life to reflect the integrity of someone who walks his talk. But I still missed the opportunity to allow my children to see the messiness of my faith journey. How valuable it would have been for them to watch God transform their own earthly daddy!

Even so, there's good news: *I am still alive, and so are my children.* Every moment of my earthly life, I have a chance to share the Good News of our Lord and Savior. I strive daily to walk my talk and allow my faith journey to be on full display. And God patiently reveals my rough edges. As He continues to invest in my growth, I can allow my children to watch my journey in real time. And now Jenni and I have grandchildren and great-grandchildren. All this is my most important legacy!

For years I've shared my faith journey as a visible part of my work. Our ministry values openness and authenticity with our clients and audiences. The gospel in its most basic form always includes some version of "Here is what God is able and willing to do in us and through us, in spite of us." That *is* good news! It's never about how awesome we are, regardless of how much God has gifted us. It is always about how awesome He is, how much He loves us, and how much He wants us to be part of His team, in spite of all our limitations and shortcomings.

The key question each of us must answer is this: Are we willing to be on God's team? If we are, there are two ways that we, as followers of Christ, can make the greatest impact on others and contribute most dramatically to His Kingdom. These are foundational components of building a powerful legacy for those closest to us, as well as the world at large.

The first significant way to leave a legacy as you invest in the Kingdom is to recognize that God created humans to be full and satisfied and to feel as if our lives really matter. This is what we all naturally long for. As Christians, we know that Jesus is our only true source of power and fulfillment. He even said that the main reason He came to earth was so that we could experience abundant life, or life "to the full" from now through eternity (John 10:10, NIV). By learning how to remain connected to Him, we prove that what we claim is theoretically possible (life in the fullness of Christ) is also true. Without that authenticity, our gospel message is really just a nice story—a fairy tale. Those around us will see it and feel it, and our claims about the benefits of Christianity become mere hype.

The single most significant thing you can contribute to the Kingdom of God is to prove through the way you live that the Good News is true—and let God fill you. You can then regularly, generously, and sacrificially invest those rich resources into the lives of others as you continually return to God and ask Him to refill you. That is what real self-care is. As the greatest commandment directs us, we are to care for others in the same way we care for ourselves (Matthew 22:39). As you do this, others will witness what you have. And when they ask you about it, inform them that it's not complicated. It's available to all who ask. Surrender your life to Christ, plug in and get filled, give generously, and then refill. That is how we were all created to live. We hope this book has provided you with some practical tools to do this well.

The second significant way to leave a legacy through your investment in the Kingdom of God is to have a healthy, fully functional, and satisfying marriage. God created us as relational beings meant to live in safe and satisfying relationships and community with others. The foundation of all this is the family, and the central relational component is marriage. Our current culture appears to be rapidly giving up on the idea that an intimate, lifelong relationship between a man and a woman in marriage is even relevant in today's world. Many people see traditional marriage as an outdated institution. Others say they don't want to get married because they've seen nothing among the married people they've observed for any length of time that has interested them or attracted them to marriage.

But we still believe that God created marriage as the cornerstone of His plan and purpose. As you learn how to build a dynamic, incredibly safe, and satisfying marriage consisting of two real friends, trusted lovers, and skillful teammates, what you create will prove once again that abundant life is possible in Christ.

Obviously, walking this out takes work, commitment, and perseverance. But it's doable, because our God is interested, willing, and able to take us there if we let Him.

Let's Continue the Journey!

As we promised at the beginning of this book, you really do have the God-given power to make your marriage the best it can be. We have personally witnessed thousands of couples grab hold of this power and transform their struggling marriages. We never tire of hearing inspiring stories of often-miraculous transformations. By God's grace, you, too, have the power to make your life and marriage the kind of love story that demonstrates to the world how amazing, faithful, and available our loving Lord really is.

Perhaps your spouse has joined you on this journey toward health and wholeness, but even if they haven't, you have all the tools at your disposal to improve yourself and your marriage step by step. We serve a powerful God, and nothing is impossible with Him (Luke 1:37)!

As you pursue a great marriage, keep aiming for the delicate balance of caring well for yourself while also caring for your spouse and marriage. Being empowered to love is God's design and intent! As you live out His purpose for your life and marriage, others will want what you have.

The grand vision we, your authors, shared at the beginning of this journey bears repeating: Our hearts' desire and prayer is that couples everywhere will learn the art of caring well for themselves and their spouses and then share those skills with others, so that marriages around the world can become glorious examples of what is possible with Christ.

Appendices

Appendix A

Spiritual Discipline Exercises

IN CHAPTER 4, we outlined a number of spiritual disciplines that can help you draw closer to God and deepen your relationship with Him. Here we offer a few sample exercises you can try during your private times with the Lord.

Solitude Exercise

Consider pulling away from the busyness of each day to spend time alone with God. You could seek out a private room in your house where no one will disturb you for half an hour, or you could drive to a local park and find a solitary place to sit. You could even go to a deserted corner of a parking lot, away from all the commotion. During this time of solitude, turn your phone and social media devices off. Let loved ones know where you are in case they need to reach you in an emergency, but commit to being unreachable for these dedicated minutes of solitude. While you're there, consider practicing one or more of the following disciplines.

Silence Exercise 1

If you're new to silence, begin with just a few minutes. In a place of solitude, turn off all generated noise (phone, music, podcasts, audiobooks, etc.) and notice the background sounds around you (birds, traffic, the ticking of a clock, etc.). Is it difficult to quiet your mind? Be patient with yourself. This is challenging to learn. When you notice yourself thinking about other things, simply bring your attention back to the moment.

Some people find it helpful to have something in particular to focus on as they learn to quiet their minds. Consider slowly repeating "Jesus" with each breath. Or breathe the Hebrew name for God (*Yahweh*) in and out: Slowly breathe in and think *Yah*; then slowly breathe out and think *weh*. Fill your lungs as you breathe in and empty them as you breathe out: *Yah-weh*.

Silence Exercise 2

The next time you feel tempted to defend yourself or explain your actions, try refraining until someone *specifically asks* for an explanation. Be prepared for the likelihood that this request will never come. So sit with *not* explaining yourself and remind yourself that your Father in heaven sees you and knows what happened. Try to release the outcome to Him and be open and curious to see how things work out when you do.

Prayer Exercise (*Lectio Divina*)

Choose a short passage of Scripture, one to ten verses long. You'll read this passage three times, or you could simply listen to it on a free Bible app, such as YouVersion. You might even consider reading the passage in a version of the Bible you are less familiar with. This can give Scripture a fresh voice and open you to new perspectives from God.

Before you begin, ask God to join you in a conversation through His Word. Have an attitude of openness and expectancy that He really does want to speak to you today. Read the passage once to familiarize yourself with it. Then during your second reading, look for a word or phrase that stands out to you. Hold it in your mind as you finish the reading, then pause and contemplate that word or phrase.

- What is God saying to you through that word or phrase?
- Does it resonate with anything going on in your life right now?
- Is there anything God wants you to be aware of?
- Is He trying to convict you of any sin?

Take as long as you like meditating on the passage and listening to God. Feel free to dialogue with Him, but remember, the primary purpose of your dialogue is to *hear* from Him. When you're ready, read the passage a final time. Be open to hearing anything God might be asking you to *do*. Take time to listen and contemplate the passage as you consider what He might be asking of you. When you're finished, simply thank Him for this time together.

Even if you didn't really hear anything, that's okay. You still practiced the discipline of being in God's presence and listening to Him. We guarantee He is pleased with your efforts. It's time well spent and gets easier with practice. Surrender the results to Him. This is about relationship, not accomplishing something.

Meditation Exercise

Choose a verse or biblical truth you can recite in one breath, such as "I belong to God," or "God is [my] refuge and strength" (Psalm 46:1), or "The God of the universe loves me deeply." Consider adding your name to the statement—for example: "I, [insert your name], can do all things through [Christ] who strengthens me" (Philippians 4:13). Set a timer for one to five minutes so you won't get distracted.

Ask God to speak to you as you meditate on His truth. Then slowly repeat this statement silently several times, aloud if you're alone. As you do, emphasize different words: "*I*, [insert your name], belong to God"; "I, [insert your name], *belong* to God"; "I, [insert your name], belong to *God*." Each time, pause and listen to what God might be speaking to your heart. Allow the words to take root. Ask God to show you this truth at a deeper level in your life. Continue to repeat the statement until your timer goes off. If you find your mind wandering to other topics, that's okay. Simply let those thoughts go and bring your attention back to your statement.

Study Exercise

Choose a relatively short book of the Bible, such as Ruth or Philippians, and commit to reading the entire book every day for a month. Ask the Holy Spirit to help you understand what you're reading. What do you think it means? What do you notice about the book's structure? Are there any repeated words or themes? Could that be significant? Is there anything in the book you struggle with? Are there portions you disagree with? Why do you suppose that is? Consider journaling your observations and reflections each day and notice how your understanding changes over thirty days. Feel free to consult Bible dictionaries, commentaries, or other writings about the book you are studying as you progress through the month. How do those resources impact your understanding of the book you're studying? Consider reading different perspectives, not just the ones you are most familiar or comfortable with. Where do you come down as you wrestle with these different interpretations? Ask the Holy Spirit to guide your reflections. Is there a verse or selection of verses you would like to memorize?

Appendix B

Reactive Cycle Exercise

RECALL TIMES WHEN YOU EXPERIENCED conflict, tension, or awkwardness as a couple. Take a few minutes to jot down your *most common conflicts*. For the sake of this exercise, imagine yourself in one or more of these conflicts as you address the following questions.

1. IDENTIFY YOUR FEARS/TRIGGERS/BUTTONS

What are the fears, triggers, or "buttons" that get pushed during conflict? What *feelings* do you experience?

Check all that apply, but place a star next to your five most common or intense feelings.

☑	Feeling	"As a result of conflict, tension, or disharmony, I'm concerned . . ."
	abandoned	my spouse will ultimately leave me, and I will be alone.
	afraid of intimacy	I am afraid of opening up emotionally to my mate or others; I will be hurt if I allow my spouse past my walls; it is uncomfortable to open up the deepest, most essential parts of who I am.
	alone	I will be by myself or on my own; I will be without help or assistance; I will be lonely and isolated.

☑ Feelings	"As a result of conflict, tension, or disharmony, I'm concerned . . ."
betrayed	my mate will be disloyal or unfaithful; my spouse has given up on the relationship; my mate will share or reveal private information with others.
controlled	I will be dominated; I will be made to submit; what my spouse says goes; I will be treated like a child, or my mate will act like my parent.
deceived	my relationship will lack truth, honesty, or trustworthiness; truth will be perverted in order to cheat or defraud me; I will be misled or deceived.
defective	something is wrong with me; I'm the problem; I am broken and unlovable.
disconnected	we will become emotionally detached or separated; there are walls or barriers between us in the marriage.
disrespected	I will be treated rudely; my thoughts and opinions will be disregarded; my mate does not respect or admire me; my spouse has a low opinion of me.
failure	I am not successful as a husband/wife; I will fall short in my relationship; I won't make the grade.
helpless/ powerless	I am unable to do anything to change my spouse or my situation; I am at the end of my power, resources, capacity, or ability to get what I want; things are unmanageable and beyond my control.
humiliated	I will be shamed, degraded, and embarrassed; my dignity and self-respect are attacked; I will be made the fool.
ignored	my spouse will not pay attention to me; I feel neglected and invisible.
inadequate	others are more competent than me; I am incapable and ineffective. I will let others down, and I will disappoint my mate.

☑	Feelings	"As a result of conflict, tension, or disharmony, I'm concerned . . ."
	inferior	everyone else is better than I am; I am less valuable or important than others.
	insignificant	I don't matter in this relationship; I will be of no consequence to my spouse; I am immaterial, not worth mentioning, trivial in the eyes of my mate.
	invalidated	who I am, what I think, what I do, or how I feel doesn't matter.
	judged	I am always being unfairly criticized or misjudged; my spouse forms faulty or negative opinions about me; I am always being evaluated.
	misportrayed	I will be portrayed inaccurately; I am described in a negative or untrue manner; my spouse paints a wrong picture of me.
	misunderstood	my spouse will fail to understand me correctly; he/she will get the wrong idea or impression about me; I will be misperceived or misread.
	not good enough	nothing I do is ever acceptable, satisfactory, or sufficient; there will always be more hoops to jump through; I won't measure up to my spouse's expectations of me.
	phony	I strongly desire to act in accord with who I say I am, yet I don't know how to reconcile the contradictions that lie within me; others will discover those contradictions within me and believe the worst.
	rejected	my spouse doesn't want to be with me and does not accept me; I will be pushed away and discarded.
	taken advantage of	I will be cheated on by my mate; I will feel like a "doormat"; my goodwill is exploited.
	unaware	I do not know what is going on in the relationship; I do not have the necessary information; I'm in the dark; I'm clueless; things feel secretive, hidden, or undisclosed.

☑	Feelings	"As a result of conflict, tension, or disharmony, I'm concerned . . ."
	unfair	I will be treated unfairly; I will be asked to do things my spouse is unwilling to do (double standard); I will be asked to do things that are unreasonable or excessive; I will be treated differently than others.
	unimportant	I am not important to my mate; I am of little or no priority to my spouse.
	unknown	I'm afraid to move forward because the outcome is uncertain; if I am not prepared, then I won't feel secure.
	unloved	my spouse doesn't love me anymore; my spouse has no affection, care, or desire for me.
	unwanted	I am not desirable; my spouse is staying in the marriage out of duty, obligation, or because it's the right thing to do.
	worthless	my value and worth are not recognized; I feel cheapened, less than, or devalued in the marriage; I have little or no value to my spouse; my mate does not see me as priceless.
	other	

Look at the feelings you starred in response to question 1. List the top five feelings you experience during conflict, tension, or disharmony.

Feeling 1 _____

Feeling 2 _____

Feeling 3 _____

Feeling 4 _____

Feeling 5 _____

2. IDENTIFY YOUR REACTIONS

What do you do when your buttons get pushed? What are the common ways you *react* when you feel what you indicated in the previous question?

Check all that apply, and then place a star next to your five most common, favorite, or most intense reactions or coping behaviors.

☑	Reactions	Explanation
	abdicate	You give away or deny your authority or responsibility.
	act out	You engage in negative behaviors like drug or alcohol abuse, extramarital affairs, excessive spending, or overeating.
	anger/rage	You display strong feelings of displeasure or violent and uncontrolled emotions.
	arrogance	You posture yourself as superior, better than, or wiser than your mate.
	avoidance	You get involved in activities to avoid your mate or certain topics.
	belittle	You devalue or dishonor someone with words or actions; you call your spouse names, use insults, ridicule, take potshots, or mock them.
	blame	You place responsibility on others, not accepting fault; you're convinced the problem is your spouse's fault.
	broadcast	You share your problems and concerns with people outside of your marriage.
	caretake	You regularly take on the burdens of others; you find it hard to rest until everyone around you is provided for; you overfunction by taking on the details, tasks, and responsibilities of others.
	catastrophize	You use dramatic, exaggerated expressions to depict that the relationship is in danger or that it has failed.

☑	Reactions	Explanation
	clinginess	You develop a strong emotional attachment or dependence on your spouse or others; you hold tight to your mate.
	complain	You readily express unhappiness or make accusations.
	control	You hold back, restrain, oppress, or dominate your mate; you rule over your spouse; you talk over or prevent your mate from having a chance to explain their position, opinions, or feelings.
	criticize	You find and verbalize fault in your mate; you bring up what is wrong and focus on negative aspects of your mate or your relationship.
	cross-complain	You often meet your mate's complaint (criticism) with an immediate complaint of your own.
	defensiveness	Instead of listening, you defend yourself by providing an explanation; you make excuses for your actions.
	demand	You try to force your mate to do something, usually with implied threat of punishment if they refuse.
	denial	You refuse to admit or you ignore the truth or reality.
	dishonesty	You lie about, fail to reveal, give out false impressions of, or falsify your thoughts, feelings, habits, likes, dislikes, personal history, daily activities, or plans for the future.
	earn-it mode	You try to do more to earn others' love and care.
	escalate	Your emotions spiral out of control; you argue, raise your voice, or fly into a rage.
	exaggerate	You make overstatements or enlarge your words beyond bounds or the truth; you make statements like "You always . . ." or "You never . . ."

☑	Reactions	Explanation
	fact-find	You actively seek the facts and details to determine what really happened; you pursue evidence to prove your point.
	fix-it mode	You focus almost exclusively on what is needed to solve or fix the problem.
	humor	You use humor as a way of not dealing with the issue at hand.
	independence	You become independent (separate from your mate) in your attitude, behavior, or decision-making.
	invalidate	You discredit your spouse's thoughts, feelings, and actions; you give no weight to your spouse's opinions and seek to nullify and refute them.
	isolate	You shut down and go into seclusion or into your "cave."
	judge	You negatively critique, evaluate, form an opinion, or conclude something about your mate.
	lecture	You sermonize, talk down to, scold, or reprimand your mate.
	manipulation	You control, influence, or maneuver your spouse for your own advantage.
	mind read	You make assumptions about your mate's private feelings, behaviors, or motives.
	minimize	You assert that your spouse is overreacting to an issue; you intentionally underestimate, downplay, or soft-pedal the issue or how they feel.
	nag	You badger, pester, or harass your mate to do something you want.
	negative beliefs	You believe your spouse is far worse than is really the case; you see your spouse in a negative light or attribute negative motives to them; you see your mate through a negative lens.

☑	Reactions	Explanation
	negative body language	Your feelings are expressed through nonverbal cues (facial expressions, tone of voice, posture, etc.) that are noticeable to all.
	pacify	You try to soothe, calm down, or placate your spouse; you try to get them to not feel negative emotions.
	passive-aggressive behavior	You display negative emotions, resentment, and aggression in passive ways, such as procrastination, forgetfulness, and stubbornness.
	personalize	You make the actions or inactions of your spouse about yourself; you interpret comments and actions as critical messages directed at you even if you are not specifically mentioned.
	pessimism	You become negative, distrustful, cynical, and skeptical in your view of your spouse and marriage.
	provoke	You intentionally aggravate, hassle, goad, or irritate your spouse.
	rationalize	You attempt to make your actions seem reasonable; you try to attribute your behavior to credible motives; you try to provide believable but untrue reasons for your conduct.
	repeat yourself	You state your own position again and again instead of understanding your mate's position.
	replay	You rewind and replay the argument over and over; you ruminate about what your mate does or doesn't do that frustrates or hurts you.
	rewrite history	You recast your earlier times together in a negative light; your recall of previous disappointments and slights becomes dramatically enhanced.
	right/wrong	You argue about who is right and who is wrong; you debate whose position is the correct or right one.

REACTIVE CYCLE EXERCISE

☑	Reactions	Explanation
	righteous indignation	You believe that you deserve to be angry, resentful, or annoyed with your spouse because of what they did.
	righteousness	You make it a moral issue by arguing about issues of morality or righteousness.
	sarcasm	You use negative or hostile humor, hurtful words, belittling comments, cutting remarks, or demeaning statements.
	self-abandon	You desert yourself; you neglect you; you take care of everyone except you.
	self-deprecate	You run yourself down or become very critical of yourself.
	selfishness	You are concerned with you and your interests, feelings, wants, or desires while disregarding or paying little heed to those of others.
	shut down	You detach emotionally and close your heart to your spouse; you numb out; you become devoid of emotion.
	stonewall	You put up walls and stop responding to your mate; you refuse to share or show any emotion.
	strike out	You lash out in anger; you become verbally or physically aggressive or abusive.
	stubborn	You will not budge from your position; you become inflexible or persistent.
	tantrums	You have a fit of bad temper; you become irritable, crabby, or grumpy.
	vent	You emotionally vomit, unload, or dump on your mate.
	victim mode	You see your spouse as an attacking monster and yourself as put-upon, unfairly accused, mistreated, or unappreciated.
	withdraw	You pull out of arguments when they become too much; once you pull out, you rarely, if ever, revisit the conflict; you get distant, sulk, or use the silent treatment.

☑	Reactions	Explanation
	withhold	You hold back your affections, feelings, sexual intimacy, or love from your spouse.
	yes, but . . .	You start out agreeing (yes) and then end up disagreeing (but).
	other	

Look at the items you starred in response to question 2. List the top five ways you react during conflict, tension, or disharmony.

Reaction 1 _____

Reaction 2 _____

Reaction 3 _____

Reaction 4 _____

Reaction 5 _____

3. IDENTIFY YOUR DESIRES

What do you truly desire, or want, in your marriage?

Check all that apply, but place a star next to your five most important desires.

☑	"I want . . ." or "I want to be . . ."	What That Feeling Sounds Like
	acceptance	I want to be warmly received for who I am without condition.
	accurately portrayed	I want to be seen correctly; I want my mate to represent me in a true and accurate manner.
	adequate	I want to feel like I measure up and am good enough.
	affection	I want to feel fondness and warmth.

REACTIVE CYCLE EXERCISE

☑	"I want . . ." or "I want to be . . ."	What That Feeling Sounds Like
	appreciation	I want what I do to be noticed, valued, and acknowledged.
	approval	I want to be liked and accepted.
	assistance	I want a helpmate; I want help, support, backing, and assistance from my spouse.
	attention	I want to be noticed and attended to.
	care	I want to know that others care about me and are interested in my well-being.
	comfort	I want to feel a sense of well-being.
	commitment	I want to have unconditional security in relationships.
	companionship	I want to enjoy spending time with my mate and they with me.
	competence	I want to have skills and ability that bring success.
	grace	I want something good (e.g., forgiveness) that I don't deserve.
	hero	I want to be the knight in shining armor, to be my mate's champion.
	hope	I want confidence that I will get what I love and desire.
	intimacy	I want to open my heart and not have walls in my marriage; I want to feel a deep closeness and connection with my mate.
	joy	I want to feel lasting satisfaction and happiness; I want to be thrilled with my marriage.
	love	I want to be loved deeply; I want to know that others experience me as lovable.
	partnership	I want to feel like I have a teammate or partner for a spouse; I want us both to share equal responsibility for our marriage.
	passion	I want excitement, fascination, intrigue, romance, and adventure.

☑	"I want . . ." or "I want to be . . ."	What That Feeling Sounds Like
	peacefulness	I want calmness, serenity, and tranquility; I want to feel relaxed in my marriage.
	power	I want to impact and influence my life and my marriage; I want to know that what I do makes a difference.
	respect	I want to be admired and esteemed.
	safety	I want to feel protected and secure.
	self-determination	I want to have independence and free will.
	significance	I want to have meaning and purpose.
	success	I want to experience a sense of achievement and accomplishment.
	support	I want others to be on my side; I want someone to be beside me through thick and thin.
	trust	I want to have faith in others and know they are reliable.
	understanding	I want to be known and understood at a deep level.
	usefulness	I want to contribute something valuable to the marriage.
	validation	I want to feel valued for who I am, what I think, and what I feel.
	wanted	I want to be sought after; I want to be desirable to my mate.
	other	

REACTIVE CYCLE EXERCISE

Look at the items you starred in response to question 3. List the top five things you want to experience as much as possible in your marriage.

Desire 1 _____

Desire 2 _____

Desire 3 _____

Desire 4 _____

Desire 5 _____

REACTIVE CYCLE
MAP

WIFE'S WANTS

HUSBAND'S BUTTONS

HUSBAND'S WANTS

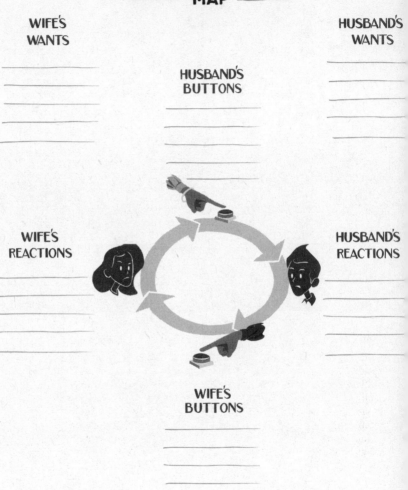

WIFE'S REACTIONS

HUSBAND'S REACTIONS

WIFE'S BUTTONS

Appendix C

Body Sensations

Pleasant Sensations	Unpleasant Sensations		
bubbly	beating/thumping	black/gray	achy
cushy	bloated	blocked	balled up
energized	burning	cavernous	dark
fluid	buzzing	chills	jerky
gentle	churning	cold	knotted
light	clammy	congested	paralyzed
loose	clenched	dense	prickly
open	constricted	distant	puffy
present	fluttery	empty	rocklike
relaxed	hot	faint	sinking
safe	itchy	fuzzy	sore
settled	nauseous	heavy	stiff
soft	pins and needles	hollow	sweaty
solid	sharp	numb	tight skin
spacious	swirling	suffocating	too big
stable	tense	thick	too small
strong		tight	trembling
tingly		tunneled	wobbly
warm		twisting	
		weak	

Appendix D

The STOP Method

WHEN PRACTICING THE AWARE STEP of the Care Cycle, some people find that their emotional or body sensations feel too intense. This could happen because they're trying to resist feeling these sensations, or it could be that the sensations feel too scary or dangerous. When sensations feel too intense, it typically indicates that we may be outside our *window of tolerance* and need to focus on neutral sensations to help us get back to a grounded ventral state.

A window of tolerance is basically another way of saying that we have slipped from our present-oriented adult brains into either fight-or-flight (protective-teen) mode or shutdown (wounded-child) mode. Learning to identify this is really the first step to getting back to your grounded state. When you become aware of being in one of these modes, you can choose to shift your focus from overwhelming distress to intentionally noticing things around you in the present moment. This will help you get back to your more mature adult state so you can safely continue the Care Cycle. Many people Tara and I (Bob) have worked with find the STOP Method helpful in these moments. Here's how the STOP Method works:

- S: *Tell yourself to stop.* Literally. Even say it aloud if you're in a place where you can. Stop spinning. Stop ramping yourself up with the negative or discouraging thoughts you are letting run through your mind. Stop looking through the eyes of the shadow monster or the hedgehog. They aren't helping you right now.

- T: *Take a deep breath* (or a couple). Breathe in for a count of four and out for a count of eight. This helps activate the calming part of the parasympathetic nervous system. Remind yourself that there is enough air around you to breathe.

- O: *Observe what is going on in this moment.* This is where you try to pay attention to things with all five of your senses (sight, hearing, smell, touch, and taste). Notice what it feels like to sit or stand where you are. How do your feet feel as you press them into the ground? Bring your attention to the contact points where your legs touch the chair or surface you're sitting on. Can you feel the sensation of your clothing on your body? What does it feel like if you move your body, even a micromovement like wiggling your big toe? Can you pick up on any smells? Consider smelling calming essential oils like lavender, mint, or orange if you have any. Try putting a piece of gum or food in your mouth and notice the tastes and sensations. Do you see any pleasant colors around you? Do you hear any sounds? Perhaps you notice movements in your body. If so, don't try to stop them; instead, see if you can intentionally slow them down. This will allow your nervous system to complete the movement in a safe way that may not have been possible in a past trauma.

- P: *Pull back and put things into perspective.* As you begin to feel calmer, remind yourself that you are an adult now, and you're allowed to feel safe when you are safe. Nothing dangerous is happening in this moment. Give yourself permission to feel that sense of safety and calm. Emotions and body sensations are information. They are not dangerous.

As you find yourself settling and becoming more grounded, you will be ready to move on to the next steps in the Care Cycle.

Appendix E

Feeling Words

Pleasant Emotions

accepted	accepting	admiration	affectionate
affirmed	agreeable	amazed	amused
appreciated	astonished	at ease	attracted
awed	belonging	blessed	blissful
bold	brave	bright	calm
captivated	carefree	certain	charmed
cheerful	cherished	clever	comforted
competent	complete	confident	content
creative	courageous	curious	daring
dazzled	delighted	determined	devoted
drawn toward	eager	ecstatic	elated
empowered	energetic	enthusiastic	excited
exhilarated	fascinated	flabbergasted	forceful
fortunate	free	frisky	giddy
glad	gleeful	grateful	hardy
hopeful	important	impulsive	inquisitive
inspired	interested	intimate	jolly

joyful	keen	known	liberated
lighthearted	longing	loving	lucky
marvelous	motivated	nostalgic	nurturing
open	optimistic	passionate	playful
pleasant	pleased	powerful	proud
provocative	receptive	relaxed	respected
responsive	rocked	safe	secure
seen	sensuous	serene	settled
shocked	stimulated	successful	surprised
tender	thankful	thoughtful	thrilled
tranquil	trusting	valuable	vibrant
victorious	warm	wonderful	worthwhile

Unpleasant Emotions

accused	aggressive	agitated	alarmed
alienated	alone	angry	annoyed
anxious	apathetic	appalled	ashamed
attacked	baffled	begrudging	bewildered
bitter	blamed	bored	cold
confused	covetous	cowardly	craving
critical	crushed	dejected	depressed
desolate	despairing	desperate	discouraged
disgusted	disinterested	disillusioned	dismayed
distant	distressed	doubtful	dread
dull	embarrassed	envious	fatigued
fear	fed up	foggy	forlorn

FEELING WORDS

frustrated	furious	greedy	grieved
guilty	hateful	heartbroken	heavy
helpless	hesitant	hopeless	horrified
hostile	humiliated	hurt	inadequate
incapable	incensed	indecisive	indifferent
indignant	inferior	infuriated	insecure
insensitive	insignificant	irritated	isolated
jealous	lifeless	lonely	lost
lustful	naive	nervous	neutral
nonchalant	numb	offended	outraged
overwhelmed	pained	panicked	paralyzed
pessimistic	preoccupied	rejected	remorseful
resentful	reserved	sad	scared
selfish	shocked	shy	skeptical
sleepy	smug	sorrowful	spiteful
stupefied	stupid	tense	terrified
threatened	timid	tired	unbelieving
uncertain	uneasy	unhappy	unpleasant
unsure	upset	vulnerable	wary
weary	worried	wronged	

Appendix F

How God Sees You

You are made in His image: "Then God said, 'Let us make man in our image, after our likeness. And let them have dominion over the fish of the sea and over the birds of the heavens and over the livestock and over all the earth and over every creeping thing that creeps on the earth.' So God created man in his own image, in the image of God he created him; male and female he created them" (Genesis 1:26-27).

You are fearfully and wonderfully made: "I praise you, for I am fearfully and wonderfully made. Wonderful are your works; my soul knows it very well" (Psalm 139:14).

You are created for God's work: "For we are his workmanship, created in Christ Jesus for good works, which God prepared beforehand, that we should walk in them" (Ephesians 2:10).

You are dead to sin and alive in Christ: "So you also must consider yourselves dead to sin and alive to God in Christ Jesus" (Romans 6:11).

You are a new creation: "Therefore, if anyone is in Christ, he is a new creation. The old has passed away; behold, the new has come" (2 Corinthians 5:17).

You are God's child: "But to all who did receive him, who believed in his name, he gave the right to become children of God" (John 1:12).

You are Jesus' friend: "No longer do I call you servants, for the servant does not know what his master is doing; but I have called you friends, for all that I have heard from my Father I have made known to you" (John 15:15).

You are set free from condemnation, sin, and death: "There is therefore now no condemnation for those who are in Christ Jesus. For the law of the Spirit of life has set you free in Christ Jesus from the law of sin and death" (Romans 8:1-2).

You are made on purpose with a purpose: "And we know that for those who love God all things work together for good, for those who are called according to his purpose" (Romans 8:28).

You are God's temple: "Do you not know that you are God's temple and that God's Spirit dwells in you?" (1 Corinthians 3:16).

You are made alive in Christ: "But God, being rich in mercy, because of the great love with which he loved us, even when we were dead in our trespasses, made us alive together with Christ— by grace you have been saved—and raised us up with him and seated us with him in the heavenly places in Christ Jesus" (Ephesians 2:4-6).

Notes

CHAPTER 2 | FOUNDATIONS OF A GREAT MARRIAGE
1. "The Serenity Prayer," attributed to Reinhold Niebuhr, quoted in "Prayer for Serenity," Celebrate Recovery, accessed October 3, 2023, https://www.celebraterecovery.com/resources/serenity-prayer.

CHAPTER 3 | IDENTITY AND PURPOSE
1. *The Karate Kid*, directed by John G. Avildsen (Culver City, CA: Columbia Pictures, 1984).
2. Ideas gleaned from Billy Graham, *The Journey: How to Live by Faith in an Uncertain World* (Nashville: W Publishing, 2006), and Loren Cunningham, *Is That Really You, God? Hearing the Voice of God* (Seattle: YWAM Publishing, 2001).

CHAPTER 4 | DISEMPOWERED TO EMPOWERED
1. Richard J. Foster, *Celebration of Discipline: The Path to Spiritual Growth* (New York: HarperCollins, 1998), 79.
2. Nathan Foster, *The Making of an Ordinary Saint: My Journey from Frustration to Joy with the Spiritual Disciplines* (Oxford: Monarch Books, 2014), 21.
3. Foster, *Celebration of Discipline*, 158.

CHAPTER 6 | WHAT DOES GOOD SELF-CARE LOOK LIKE?
1. Dr. Greg Smalley and Erin Smalley, *Reconnected: Moving from Roommates to Soulmates in Your Marriage* (Colorado Springs: Focus on the Family, 2020).
2. Daniel Goleman, *Emotional Intelligence: Why It Can Matter More Than IQ* (New York: Bantam, 2006), xxii.
3. Deb Dana, *The Polyvagal Theory in Therapy: Engaging the Rhythm of Regulation* (New York: W. W. Norton, 2018), 164.

CHAPTER 7 | FORGIVENESS AND FREEDOM

1. Mayo Clinic staff, "Forgiveness: Letting Go of Grudges and Bitterness," Healthy Lifestyle, Mayo Clinic, November 22, 2022, https://www.mayo clinic.org/healthy-lifestyle/adult-health/in-depth/forgiveness/art-20047692.

2. Everett L. Worthington Jr., "Forgiving the Man Who Murdered My Mom," *Christianity Today*, August 29, 2013, https://www.christianitytoday.com /ct/2013/september/forgiving-man-who-murdered-my-mom.html.

3. Based on a list originally developed by Dr. Tat-Ying Wong, "Seven Steps to Genuinely Forgive Your Offender," posted by Melinda Estabrooks, *Motivational Mondays* (blog), SeeHearLove.com, January 21, 2018, https://seehearlove.com/motivational-mondays/seven-steps-genuinely -forgive-offender.

CHAPTER 8 | BEING GOOD TOGETHER

1. "The Serenity Prayer," attributed to Reinhold Niebuhr, quoted in "Prayer for Serenity," Celebrate Recovery, accessed October 3, 2023, https://www .celebraterecovery.com/resources/serenity-prayer.

2. Robert S. Paul, *Finding Ever After: A Romantic Adventure for Her, An Adventurous Romance for Him* (Minneapolis: Bethany House, 2007), 155–57.

MARRIAGE
Getaways™
BY **FOCUS ON THE FAMILY**

MAKE YOUR MARRIAGE
FEEL BRAND-NEW

Refresh your relationship at a Focus on the Family Marriage Getaway. Relax in a beautiful setting away from your stressful schedule. Learn new tools from our certified Christian counseling team. Go home with a stronger bond.

LEARN MORE:

FocusOnTheFamily.com/Getaway

MARRIAGE Assessment
BY FOCUS ON THE FAMILY

Keep Growing Your Marriage.

Find your strengths – and opportunities for growth – with the Focus on the Family Marriage Assessment! You and your spouse will get a detailed report on ways to make your marriage even stronger. You'll also get resources that will help you deepen your bond.

Take the Assessment at
FocusOnTheFamily.com/MarriageAssessment